*The Entrance*

Composite drawing of the front doorway of the Octagon, with some details shown in larger scale and superimposed—an *analytique* in the *Beaux Arts* tradition.                    *Glenn Brown*

Soffit of Arch
scale

Profile of Arch

Profile of Carriage Stairs

Handrail

Profile of Chair Rail

Profile of Base Board

Nosing

Soffit of Cornice · Capital & Base
scale

Details of Entrance Hall
Scale

Stove and Newel
scale

Detail of Plaster Cornice
scale

# OCTAGON

BEING AN ACCOUNT OF A FAMOUS WASHINGTON
RESIDENCE: ITS GREAT YEARS, DECLINE & RESTORATION

BY GEORGE McCUE

AMERICAN INSTITUTE OF ARCHITECTS FOUNDATION

WASHINGTON, D.C.

1976

Copyright © 1976 by The American Institute of Architects Foundation

FRONT COVER:

The Octagon in 1889, a decade before it was occupied by the American Institute of Architects; detail of a watercolor by A. Harkness

*Government Services Savings and Loan Association, Bethesda, Maryland*

INSIDE FRONT AND BACK COVERS:

Surveyor Andrew Ellicott's Plan of Washington, engraved in 1792, with the diagonal main streets named and the squares marked with assigned numbers.

# CONTENTS

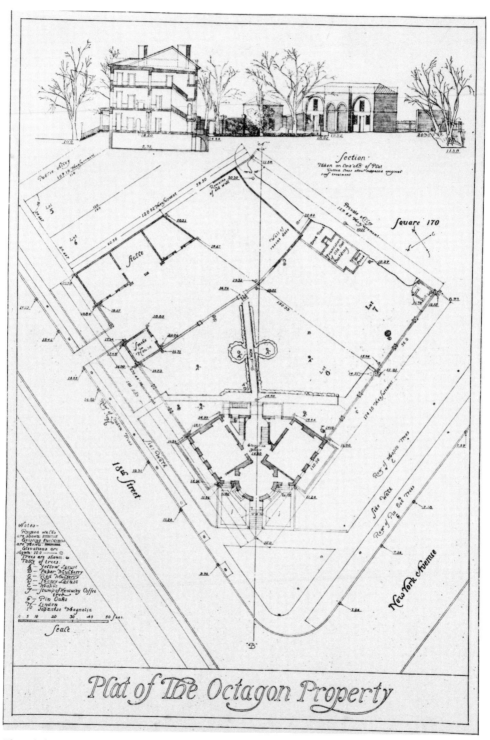

Plat of the Octagon property as measured in 1914. The east boundary of the original purchase, Lot 8, is the line extended from the irregular right-side stable wall. Stable and smokehouse designs are shown in elevations at top, as viewed from the south.

*Glenn Brown*

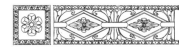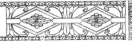

# INTRODUCTION

Old houses are memories of past times and departed personalities. As long-established images in the scenes of town and countryside they confer identity on their localities, and they become part of the lore of human society.

Old houses are documents—of site planning, construction techniques, building materials, residential design, decoration, social attitudes, personal priorities and ways of living. Many old houses serve creditably as local color, and a few are recognized as landmarks of exceptional importance to our cultural comprehensions.

For most of us the outstanding value of a well-presented landmark house is the sense of national ancestry that it affords those who approach it in search of some aspect of the early vision, the present reality and the future promise of that complex entity called the United States of America. A historic house is a cultural treasure, and a part of every citizen's patrimony.

This book is about the Octagon, designed by William Thornton and built as a winter season town house in the raw new City of Washington by John Tayloe III, a tobacco planter and breeder of race horses in Richmond County, Virginia. After the War of 1812 it became a year-around residence for some of his family. When the Octagon was built, the new capital was undergoing severe trials in the efforts begun by President Washington and carried on by the District Commissioners to attract residents and to win acceptance for the district as the national seat of government. Tayloe's decision to construct not just a part-time dwelling but a fine town house a short distance west of the still unfinished President's House—in an area then largely farmlands and woods—amounted to a heartening expression of confidence that the new community would indeed become a city.

The history of the Octagon, an early example of the urbane Adam/Federal style, is closely intertwined with the background of an earlier Tayloe house, Mount Airy, the stately Georgian home place in Richmond County. Mount Airy was built when the Tidewater region of the Virginia colony was the preserve of splendid estates built on vast landholdings originally granted by the King, or by the colonial governor in the King's name, to members of a transplanted English aristocracy. Members of the Tayloe family still occupy Mount Airy, as they have for more than two centuries. There is something marvelous in such continuity, and in the fact that both houses are eloquent documents, each of its own time and place, from the period of this country's national and cultural beginnings.

The Octagon has special interest and significance for its many independent values, but these gain perspective in its architectural relationship with Mount Airy, and in the relationship of both houses with the American turning point from a cluster of colonies to a nation.

Mount Airy speaks for the feudal landholding system under which Virginia was first developed by English gentlemen, inwardly focussed on their remote estates and in accord with a court policy of not encouraging the growth of towns in the tobacco country.

Their development of common interest with other plantation owners and farmers brought a successor generation who were more Virginians than English colonials, and their sons grew into the transcendent role of Revolutionary statesmen who were more Americans than Virginians.

The experience of this later generation at managing big estates counted strongly in the administration of a newly minted government. These men articulated and legislated and fought for the new conceptions of personal liberty, self-determination and equal opportunity that are embodied in the Declaration of Independence and the Constitution, which they helped to write. Some of the most dynamic expressions of the dignity of man to be assimilated as American principles came from the background of the aristocratic plantations of Tidewater Virginia.

The Octagon came out of that background too, but as an architectural departure, a statement of the independent spirit of the new republic, discovering the means of an American art of design in a house specifically intended to be in a city and to be harmonious with future close neighbors.

In their journeys back and forth between Mount Airy and the Octagon, the Tayloes were covering a fairly short distance in physical transport, but a great distance in the conceptions of human society that those two houses represented—they were crossing and recrossing a long bridge between an imposed class system and a system in which class was more a descriptive term than a restrictive condition.

When the American Institute of Architects bought the Octagon in 1902 for its headquarters, after having rented it for four years, the intention was to repair and restore it, the building having survived two decades of office, commercial and school rentals and approximately two more as a tenement with surprisingly little damage.

For 70 years, from 1898 to 1968, the stages of rehabilitation were paid for and supervised by the AIA. In 1968 the American Institute of Architects Foundation purchased the Octagon, and completed the restoration as it now stands. The Foundation commissioned this publication, with support by grants from the AIA

College of Fellows and the National Endowment for the Humanities, Division of Research.

There was no obligation, expressed or implied, to deal with the Octagon or the AIA role in its restoration in any way except to make this account as comprehensive and objective as possible. Any expressions of opinion are the writer's own, unless otherwise attributed, and any that reflect admiration of the AIA for seeing the Octagon project through many trials and hard decisions are gratuitous.

This effort is deeply in debt to several members of the Tayloe family and to archives of the family papers, in addition to the sources of material enumerated in the picture credits and bibliography. The Virginia Historical Society permitted quoting from its Tayloe Family Papers some of the correspondence of John Tayloe III in connection with the Octagon's construction, and from his business records. Mrs. Edward Thornton Tayloe, of Charlottesville, permitted quotations of material relating to the Tayloe estate from family papers on loan to the University of Virginia Library. To the prodigious research of W. Randolph Tayloe of Berryville, Virginia, this account is obligated for many an elusive fact and date from his geneology of the Mount Airy and Octagon families. Mrs. René Maurice Stéphan, of Columbia, South Carolina, permitted quotations from the reminiscences of her great aunt, Virginia Tayloe Lewis; she also filled in dates and personal details of the John Tayloe III family from her contemporary records, into which she dug patiently and repeatedly so that the children of this family could be identified in order of birth with other data for the enumeration in the Appendix, here published for the first time. Colonel and Mrs. Henry Gwynne Tayloe Jr., the present owners of Mount Airy, hospitably conducted a tour of their house and grounds, and their son, Henry Gwynne Tayloe III, provided many details of early Tayloe history from his own research.

The manuscript was reviewed by David N. Yerkes, FAIA, President of the American Institute of Architects Foundation; Francis D. Lethbridge, FAIA, J. Everette Fauber Jr., FAIA, Robert Garbee, AIA, Jeanne F. Butler, Administrator, AIA Foundation and Curator of the Octagon, and Elinor E. Stearns, former Assistant to the Administrator. The editing is by Simpson F. Lawson, the book design by Gerard Valerio. The majority of photographs for this publication were taken by William Edmund Barrett. To all, warm thanks. The author, of course, assumes final responsibility.

GEORGE McCUE

St. Louis, Missouri
1976

# THE OCTAGON

Dr. William Thornton (*left*), the physician and self-trained architect who designed the Octagon, and his client, Colonel John Tayloe III. The portraits, by Charles de Saint Memin, are in the Octagon dining room. *American Colonization Society*

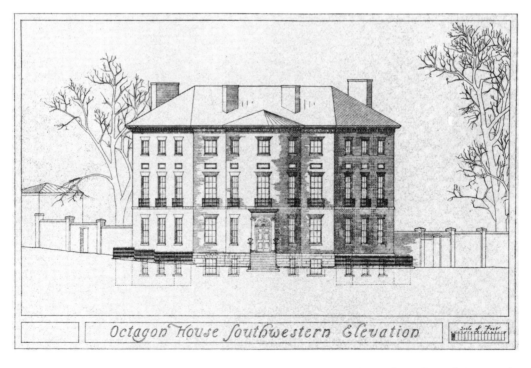

Front sides of the Octagon, in a somewhat flattened elevation that shows the Eighteenth Street side and wall, with smokehouse, at left, and the New York Avenue side at right. *Brown*

2

# ONE MAN'S HOUSE
# AND THE
# VISION OF THE FEDERAL CITY

In the 1790s the Tayloes of Mount Airy began to think about a house in town for the winter seasons. For more than a century Tayloe families had spent their lifetimes on their plantation in Richmond County, first in the seventeenth century Old House and, after 1758, in the Georgian mansion where Tayloes still live on a hilltop on the north bank of the Rappahannock River. The eldest son of each generation had inherited the plantation, in accordance with the English law of primogeniture. The first of the sons to assume the proprietorship of Mount Airy after the American Revolution was Colonel John Tayloe III, who came of age in 1792 and who enlarged on his father's eminence as an importer and breeder of notable race horses.

Through the colonial years Virginia had few towns. Social activities of the Tidewater gentry were confined to such diversions as dances, dinners, picnics, bowling on the green, river excursions and riding—very especially riding—with their social peers through their own woodlands and their own vast acreages of tobacco land. The plantation families were large and generally well acquainted with one another; their intermarriages make Virginia genealogy a fascinating maze of near and distant cousins.

Richmond County is in the Northern Neck, the long finger of land that reaches toward Chesapeake Bay between the Potomac and the Rappahannock rivers. The only town of consequence in the Northern Neck was—and is—Fredericksburg. In colonial Virginia, Williamsburg and Richmond were the only other large communities. Baltimore and Philadelphia were the nearest metropolitan centers. John Tayloe III and his wife, Ann Ogle Tayloe, whose father, Benjamin Ogle, was the Governor of Maryland at the time of their marriage, must have considered Baltimore, and perhaps Annapolis, as possibilities for a town house, but Philadelphia was the town they finally had in mind.

Mrs. Tayloe may have mentioned this to her friend, Nelly Custis, Martha Washington's granddaughter, who may have mentioned it to George Washington, who had had a warm friendship with Tayloe's father. One way or another Washington got wind of the town house, and persuaded the Tayloes to build it in the new capital city. The decision may have been abetted by Mrs. Tayloe's interest in seeing more of Nelly, then living at Mount Vernon.

On April 19, 1797, Tayloe paid $1,000 to Gustavus W. Scott for Lot 8 in Square 170, at the corner of New York Avenue and Eighteenth Street, Northwest, as laid out in a plan by Major Pierre Charles L'Enfant and surveyed by Andrew Ellicott. Scott was one of the first purchasers of lots in the newly platted capital.

Exactly two years later, on April 19, 1799, Dr. William Thornton wrote to George Washington (by then returned to private life at Mount Vernon): "Mr. J. Tayloe, of Virginia, has contracted to build a house in the City near the President's Square of $13,000 value." This begins the known documentation of the Octagon and of Thornton's connection with it: Thornton, the self-trained architect who had won the United States Capitol competition, and was then serving also as a District Commissioner. Tayloe was then 28 years of age, Thornton 40.

Washington's effort to attract the Tayloes to the Federal City was a part of his vast enterprise, attended with considerable anxiety, of establishing a new United States capital in a tract that was part woodland, part marsh and part farmland occupied by a scattering of plantations.

The Residence Act of 1790 authorized the selection of a site no more than 10 miles square in the Potomac region for the new capital. President Washington was to choose the site, acquire the land and appoint District Commissioners. His difficult objectives were to persuade the 19 landholders to agree to the dispersal of their estates, oversee the preparation of a city plan that the Congress would support, do his best to keep land speculation to a minimum, and see that a "suitable" Capitol and President's House were ready by the first Monday in December, 1800, all specified in the Residence Act. Until that time the seat of government would be at Philadelphia.

The commissioners determined, in 1791, to call the district the "Territory of Columbia," and the federal city the "City of Washington." They had expected to begin with a fairly compact area within the district as the nucleus of a seat of government, but L'Enfant's conception provided for an entire city. It presented a block-by-block plan for development all the way from Rock Creek, the east border of Georgetown, to the Anacostia River, or the Eastern Branch as it was better known then.

The site for the Capitol building was located with great care. In his survey of this tract, Ellicott established the meridian line by celestial observation, the east-west crossing by a transit instrument, the acute angles by actual measurement "and left nothing to the uncertainty of the compass." The Capitol was to stand on a height that had long been called Jenkins Hill, although that name still has not been traced to any previous owner.

A mile northwest, about midway to Georgetown, another eminence was reserved for the President's House. The grand thoroughfare that the survey showed between these key buildings and extending on to Georgetown—later Pennsylvania Avenue—was platted 160 feet wide, as were other diagonal avenues. Streets leading to public buildings or markets were to be 130 feet wide, all others 90 or 110 feet. The narrower streets were laid out in a grid, with connectors meeting (sometimes clumsily) at the circles and squares where the diagonals converged. The scheme provided for miles of majestic avenues, spendid government buildings, fine residential streets, shopping and market districts, and cultural amenities, offering, as L'Enfant wrote to Washington, "a variety of situation unparalleled in point of beauties—suitable to every purpose and in every point convenient."

All this overlaid, in a prodigious exercise of the mind's eye, a sylvan landscape that had been only lightly touched by the implements of man.

The Potomac's main channel was on the Virginia side from the mouth of Rock Creek to the Eastern Branch. On the city side, what are now West and East Potomac Parks and the Lincoln Memorial grounds were tidal flats and mud banks with shallow channels. The river flowed within a short distance of where the Washington Monument now stands, and lapped at the southwest corner of the present Ellipse.

At this point the Tiber Creek emptied into the Potomac. This little stream, known in an earlier time as Goose Creek, was renamed by Francis Pope, who in 1663 was granted much of the land west of Jenkins Hill—the present Mall area and the south part of the White House grounds. Apparently unable to resist a droll conceit (or was it a prescience of the capital to come!) Pope called his estate Rome and his creek the Tiber.

The placid Tiber, which proved capable of damaging floods, was fed by several tributaries from the northeast. It was navigable by small boats in its lower channel, about where Constitution Avenue is now. It flowed past the surveyors' stakes of the President's House grounds, and it was to be developed both as a scenic feature of a "grand walk" from the Capitol to the Potomac (the future Mall) and as a canal for barges hauling construction materials. The canal was to turn south near the Capitol and continue in two branches to the Eastern Branch. L'Enfant even proposed that the Tiber's tributary waters be channeled beneath the Capitol to a spectacular emergence from the west side of the hill as a cascade 100 feet wide with a 40-foot drop. This was never attempted.

The new republic was desperately short of money. It couldn't afford to buy 100 square miles of land for a capital, let alone pay for government buildings and a cascade. Within the government and out in the new-born states there was strong opposition to the capital's location on the Potomac; there were those who wanted it elsewhere, and others who did not want a national capital anywhere. Washington and his staff needed a persuasive show of results.

It seemed feasible that the sale of lots could finance a large part of the cost of the first government buildings and street construction. President Washington had arranged with the district landholders that each would retain every other lot within his original boundaries and donate the remaining ground to the government. They would be paid £25, or $66.66 an acre for lots used for government purposes, but not for ground to be dedicated for streets or squares. The landowners' profits from the sales of lots they retained, which were expected to rise in value, were to compensate them for the loss of their estates, and the government's profits from sales of its 10,136 lots were to undergird financing of the first federal buildings.

There was widespread doubt that the capital city could survive the disputes over what many politicians considered an extravagantly grandiose plan, and over the concept of a federation of states with a central government. It was hard to envision the raw landscape transformed into the magnificent capital of L'Enfant's description, so there was no rush to buy lots or to build on those already purchased.

The temperamental L'Enfant delayed the printing of a plan showing block locations because, he warned, its publication would encourage speculation. This was blamed for the disappointing result of a government auction of city lots in 1791—only 35 lots were sold—but not many more were sold at a second auction a year later when the plan was available.

In 1793 a land syndicate formed by James Greenleaf, Robert Morris and James Nicholson agreed to buy large packages of lots at reduced prices in return for a loan to the government of $2,200 a month until the Capitol and the President's House were completed. They agreed also to build 10 houses each year for seven years, but they went bankrupt in 1797.

Virginia and Maryland had donated $120,000 and $72,000, respectively, toward improvement costs. Several attempts to get foreign loans failed. In response to a plea by President Washington late in 1796, Maryland made a loan of $100,000, but with the ignominious requirement that the commissioners pledge their personal credit as well as that of the government.

That was the year in which Francis Baily, a visiting Englishman, wrote:

*The private buildings go on but slowly. There are about twenty or thirty houses built near the Point [confluence of the Potomac and Anacostia rivers], as well as a few in south Capitol Street and about a hundred others scattered over in other places: in all I suppose about two hundred: and these constitute the great city of Washington. The truth is, that not much more than one-half the city is cleared:—the rest is in woods; and most of the streets which are laid out are cut through these woods. . .*

Creating the city and putting it in readiness to begin functioning as the United States capital in 1800 was one of the pressing concerns of Washington's presidency and the last years of his life, against an undercurrent of talk that the government might not, at the last minute, even move from Philadelphia.

He considered it extremely important that the new capital be not only well and beautifully constructed as the seat of the national government, but that it be a pleasant environment of homes and urban attractions. Moving from exhortation to example, he bought several lots at one of the auctions to encourage other bidders. With William Thornton as agent and consultant, he commissioned a double house, later called the Hotel Kenmore, on North Capitol Street between B and C streets, where 20 or 30 members of Congress could rent rooms. He invested "between 15 and 16 thousand dollars" in this building.

Much of Washington's talent for public affairs was in the exercise of patient and persistent leadership against heavy odds, and this was decidedly the case in his establishment of the capital. There were many who had not regarded the American chances of winning the Revolution as a good bet, and despite that victory their skepticism was now transferred to the floundering new government, with its obvious tendencies to pull in various directions under its heavy burden of unfamiliar policy-making, administrative problems and emerging differences of political philosophy.

Washington made it clear that he saw the founding of the capital city as a symbol of the national identity of the United States, and as a proclamation to the world of the new republic's unified intention to succeed. One by one, the capital city lots had to be sold and built upon, and all these pieces put together to represent something new under the sun in the relationship of man with his government.

He must have imparted something of this inspiration to Colonel Tayloe, along with convincing persuasion that the woodland with only about 200 dwellings scattered along barely usable streets was a good bet for a town house. Tayloe, whose record showed him to be at home with ventures, whether in land or at the race track, commissioned what was to be for years the finest private residence in the city that was yet to come.

John Tayloe III, who commissioned the building of the Octagon. *Smithsonian Institution*

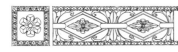 

# TWO

# THE TAYLOES
# OF COLONIAL VIRGINIA

John Tayloe III was born September 3, 1771, at Mount Airy, in the Virginia plantation house built by his father on the estate founded by his great grandfather. The third John Tayloe, born before the Revolution, was a fourth-generation American.

The first of this English family in the colony was William Tayloe, who is shown in patent books and other records to have been in Virginia by 1638, to have been a merchant and "High Sherriffe" in York County, to have bought a property called Utimaria in 1640, and to have owned an estate in Gloucester County called Rocabock.

He had a nephew, a younger William Tayloe from whom the branch of the family associated with Mount Airy and the Octagon traces its lineage. This William Tayloe, descended from a Gloucestershire family, was born in 1645, and lived in London before sailing for Virginia. No record has been found as to when he reached Virginia, but he is known to have purchased land on the north side of the Rappahannock River in 1682 from William Fauntleroy. This property was referred to at first as Tayloe's Quarter, but later was given the name by which both the estate and the present house are known today—Mount Airy.

He built a house that has been tentatively dated 1683, and in 1685 was married to Anne Corbin, daughter of Henry and Alice Corbin of Middlesex County.

John Tayloe, the first of their two sons, was born February 15, 1687. He was married to Elizabeth Gwyn Lyde, widow of Stephen Lyde; she was the daughter of David Gwyn and Catherine Griffin Fauntleroy Gwyn—her mother being the widow of the William Fauntleroy from whom William Tayloe had bought his land. Anne Corbin Tayloe died in 1694 and William Tayloe in 1710, following a second marriage.

John Tayloe I inherited Mount Airy, and built up additional large holdings in Charles County, Maryland, and in Essex and Prince William counties, Virginia. After his death September 17, 1747, the estate passed to his oldest son, John Tayloe II. The second John Tayloe was born May 8, 1721, and was married July 11, 1747, to Rebecca Plater, whose father, George Plater II, was later the Maryland

9

The Tayloe House at Williamsburg, on Nicholson Street, purchased by John Tayloe II for occupancy during sessions of the King's Council. The office is next to the house, the kitchen building beyond.

*Colonial Williamsburg Foundation*

Secretary of State, and whose brother, George Plater III, became the Governor of Maryland in 1792.

The house built by William Tayloe was destroyed by fire, possibly about 1740, although the family has found no records to support a date either for its construction or destruction. John Tayloe II built the mansion that now stands at Mount Airy on a different site from that of the Old House, as it is commonly referred to, on a hilltop overlooking the Rappahannock River valley. It was completed in 1758 after 10 years of construction.

A year later Tayloe bought what is still identified as the Tayloe House at Williamsburg, on Nicholson Street, for use during sessions of the King's Council. For this newly built residence he paid James Carter, a surgeon and apothecary, £600, an amount that still raises eyebrows in the guidebooks because it was an unusually large amount in those days for a frame house, and was triple the cost to Carter. When this house was restored in 1950, after nearly 200 years of use, considerable original material, including interior paneling, was found to be in good condition. It has two large rooms on each floor, each with a corner fireplace in a chimney centered in the outside wall. A separate office with a graceful ogee roof stands just east of the house, with the kitchen-laundry beyond.

Each of these owners of Mount Airy served on the King's Council, an elite group of citizens appointed by the governor as the upper house of the colonial General Assembly; members of the lower House of Burgesses were elected from each county. With the governor presiding, the Council became the General Court, the highest tribunal. The Assembly met first at Jamestown, the colonial capital until 1699, and then at Williamsburg.

John Tayloe II died April 19, 1779, and the estate passed to his only son, the eighth child in a family of nine children—John Tayloe III, who was eight years of age at the time of his father's death. The will of John Tayloe II appointed 11 executors and guardians, most of them prominent in Virginia history. They were his brothers-in-law Richard Corbin, Mann Page and George Plater; his nephews John Tayloe Corbin, Mann Page III and Warner Lewis Jr.; his sons-in-law Edward Lloyd IV, Francis Lightfoot Lee and Ralph Wormeley V, with Colonel William Brockenbrough and Thomas Lawson, an iron agent.

John Tayloe III was educated at Eton and Cambridge, and his marriage to Ann Ogle was in 1792. In 1799 he was commissioned a major of light dragoons by President John Adams. Like his father and grandfather, he headed the Richmond County militia, with the rank of colonel. He served for nine years as a Federalist delegate and senator in the Virginia Legislature. He ran for Congress on the Federalist ticket in 1799, and was defeated. Colonel and Mrs. John Tayloe III had 15 children, of whom four predeceased the parents. One of these was their first-born, John Tayloe IV. He died at Mount Airy in 1824 of wounds received in the War of 1812, as a midshipman on the Constitution in its historic battle with the British frigate Guerriere.

The Tayloe generations of the seventeenth and eighteenth centuries were eminently a part of that remarkable social, political and economic system, the

11

plantation of colonial Virginia, which left deep imprints on this nation's history.

"Virginia" originally was the name of English North America—all the territory not claimed by France or Spain. The first permanent breach in this wilder-
ness was Jamestown, founded in 1607, under a charter by King James I to the
Virginia Company of London. This private corporation was authorized to colonize
the part of Virginia 200 miles north and 200 miles south of what is now Old
Point Comfort.

The Virginia Company was created as a corporate overlordship of farm
estates, to be operated for the profit of the stockholders, some of whom were
"adventurers of the purse" in England, others "adventurers of the person" in the
New World. The company offered a number of arrangements for acquiring land—
through stock ownership, by investment of a share of the profits from work on a
company plantation, by arranging a mortgage with an estate owner, or by serving
under indenture as bondsman to an estate owner and then working independently.

The conveyance of property was radically changed from the system in England. Under England's feudal manorial tradition, the concept of landholding had
taken on a sacred character in an unshakeable hierarchy—the King holding land
by the grace of God, the proprietor by grace of the King, and the freeholder by
grace of the proprietor—the proprietor being the overlord of a large estate and
the freeholder usually a farmer on the estate. As acknowledgement of his inferior
title, the freeholder paid a small annual fee, a quit-rent, to the proprietor who, in
turn, paid a quit-rent to the King or performed equivalent service. An estate was
kept indivisible and handed down through the succession of eldest sons, under
the rules of primogeniture and entail. It was unthinkable that land be subject to
the market.

The idea of independent title to land was slowly taking hold in England, but
in the colony the Virginia Company accomplished this evolution quickly, while
retaining structural elements of the old hierarchy. The company's charter gave it
overlord status, and there were still social levels of those with much land, little
land and no land. The significant difference was that the company could convey
land titles in fee simple, with no quit-rents to be paid. A farmer could buy acreage, or he could work for it through encumbrance to an estate owner, but once he
took title he was an independent owner.

The company was empowered to establish a local government, and in 1619
it created the Virginia General Assembly, with a governor, an advisory council,
a secretary and a treasurer all appointed by the company managers, but also with
the first popularly elected governmental body on the American continent—the
House of Burgesses, with two members from each of the then 11 duly con-
stituted plantations, and later from each county.

Like other English kings yet to be born, James became irritated at the colon-
ists' growing self-management, which was becoming a talking point for increased
political rights for British subjects at home. In 1624 the King's Bench revoked the
company's charter. Virginia was made a royal colony from what is now Pennsylvania to Florida, and James took the first steps, shortly before his death the next

Ann Ogle Tayloe                                          *Smithsonian Institution*

year, toward a reversion of the colony to the feudal system. He appointed his own governor and a new council, and the crown became in Virginia, as it was in England, the only source of land titles.

Charles I reinforced the feudal system in America through grants of huge proprietorships taken from Virginia territory—the Carolina grant to Sir Robert Heath in 1629, and the Maryland grant in 1632 to Lord Baltimore, both Cavaliers. Many other Cavaliers—landed aristocracy who were members of the court party —emigrated to Virginia to escape punitive action by Cromwell's Roundheads in the English civil war. They were either granted land by the governor or bought it from established proprietors.

During the reign of Charles II (1660–85), Cavaliers came over in greater numbers to establish plantations on land granted by the king as reward for their fidelity to the Restoration. Many of these were younger sons who could not inherit land in England. All were transplanted Englishmen, devoted to their king, their country seats and their exclusiveness, and their plantation life was modeled as nearly as possible on that of the feudal manors where they were born.

They took up the already flourishing cultivation of tobacco, a profitable, easily transported product that had become the equivalent of money in the colony and the principal medium of exchange for English manufactured goods in a nearly closed-circuit economy. The land they favored was the loamy coastal plain, the Tidewater region, where the ocean tides flow in the rivers and tributaries for some 80 to 120 miles inland to the Piedmont Province, the next topographical step. The demarcation between upland fresh water and tidal salt water is the fall line, literally the location of falls and rapids in the four main rivers—the James, York, Rappahannock and Potomac. In some areas, the fall line became a status boundary between the Tidewater gentry and the Piedmont farmers.

The crown's proprietary grants were jurisdictions, in which the proprietors could establish their own estates and make their own conveyances of land—to another proprietorship, to a freehold with title subordinate to the estate, or to a tenancy with no title. The freeholder paid quit-rent to the proprietor, and the proprietor to the king. Subsequent Assembly enactments made some revisions in this system, but its main structure stood until after the Revolution.

Charles II, who was busy with affairs of the homeland and the other American colonies, seems to have made some grants absent-mindedly. Soon after taking the throne, he awarded jurisdiction of the Northern Neck—the long peninsula between the Potomac and Rappahannock rivers—to seven members of his court, among them Thomas, Lord Culpeper. This token of royal esteem extended from Chesapeake Bay to the source of the Potomac in the Allegheny Mountains. A later survey showed that it embraced some 5,282,000 acres, more than 8,000 square miles.

Ten years later the King nonchalantly granted the entire Virginia colony jointly to the Earl of Arlington and to Culpeper for a 31-year term, during which they were privileged to make grants, convey titles and collect quit-rents. This threw the existing landholding conditions into confusion, and the other proprietors protested vigorously through the General Assembly against the new grant superimposed on grants already made to them. The King retracted, except for the Northern Neck grant, which remained in effect. Culpeper acquired the other interests in this domain, the largest in the colony by far, and it was inherited by his grandson, Thomas, Lord Fairfax. He kept jurisdiction until the proprietary was abolished by the General Assembly in 1786.

Some of the largest and wealthiest plantations of the colony were subdivisions of the Culpeper-Fairfax domain, many of them spread over several thousand acres and a few comprising around 100,000 acres. Second only to Lord Fairfax was his land agent, Robert "King" Carter, an energetic autocrat who by the time of his death in 1732 had built up various holdings of a million acres or so in all, and had erected a splendid residence, Corotoman, overlooking the Rappahannock River near the tip of the peninsula. "King" Carter paid for the construction of Christ Church, completed in the year of his death and still an outstanding landmark in Lancaster County, in the parish where the Carters signed the vestry minute book ahead of the rector. He served as speaker of the House of Burgesses, treasurer of the colony and acting governor. He caused a road to be built for the length of the Northern Neck, from his house to Fredericksburg, connecting other plantations along approximately the present route of State Highway 3. This was jocularly called the King's Highway in recognition of the prodigious manipulation he must have exerted to get it, although the road that officially bore that name was the one to Williamsburg.

The Cavaliers needed large acreages because they were unskilled at land management. Tobacco soon depletes the soil. The smaller farmers rotated tobacco with other crops, but on the big plantations the practice was to grow three or four tobacco crops on a portion of the acreage, and then let this land "go to thicket" for about 15 years of natural replenishment, with the tobacco shifted to another tract. The estates needed more labor than indentured hands and tenants could provide, so slaves became part of the Virginia way of life.

Towns were slow to develop in colonial Virginia. Manufacturing was prohibited for years to keep the colony in the position of supplier of raw materials for English manufactures which were to be traded for tobacco. The court did not encourage town-building because towns tended to become concentrations of middle-class workers and merchants, who tended to become politically restless.

For plantation owners towns were unnecessary because their estates were relatively self-sufficient. Their slave craftsmen included, as one reminiscence put it, "carpenters, coopers, sawyers, blacksmiths, tanners, curriers, shoemakers, spinners, weavers, and knitters, and even a distiller." Seagoing ships could navigate the deep Tidewater rivers, picking up tobacco and delivering goods from English and Scotch merchants at wharves near most plantation houses, so there was no need for ports. Even the family burial place was on the plantation. The Virginians became so much conditioned to their sequestered splendor that towns made them uncomfortable. Many young men never saw a town until their first visit to Williamsburg.

Mount Airy, South lawn, ca. 1758.                    *Wm. Edmund Barrett*

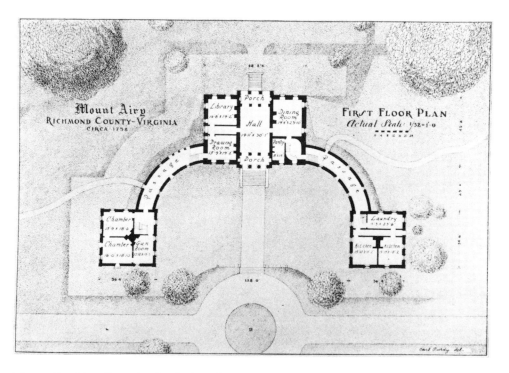

Mount Airy, First floor plan by Carl Purdy          *Wm. Edmund Barrett*

# MOUNT AIRY

The combination of intuition, judgment, reason and design sense that achieves a happy suitability of a building to its site is grandly evident at Mount Airy. On the approach by U.S. Route 360—over the long bridge from Tappahannock and then across flat bottomland—the four chimneys and roof structure are viewed in massive profile on a hilltop in the distance straight ahead. The highway swerves around and up the hill. Soon a side road leads to a private lane through woods and meadows, and the house with its flanking dependencies comes into focus.

It is the classic approach to the hall of a chieftain or a nobleman's manor—the commanding eminence and exposed grounds contributing to security in the more ancient application, and in colonial Virginia affording opportunity for the equipages of oncoming visitors to be recognized, and an estimate made of the number of plates to add to the table.

The main axis of the house is north and south, and this approach is from the north, opposite the river side. The building reveals itself as a two-story rectangle of dark stone, with a lighter stone trim. Two chimneys are at each end of a short ridge in the hip roof. The symmetrically placed dependencies stand well forward of the house, and are connected with it by curved enclosed passages. They are matching two-story buildings, lower than the house and constructed of the same dark stone. Each has a central stone chimney at the peak of a hip roof.

The house and dependencies stand on a low constructed plateau—quite an earth-moving project for a house in rural eighteenth-century Virginia—that extends, on the side facing the river valley, toward the brow of the hill in broad terraces that once supported a formal garden and a bowling green. A depression was left at the west end of the house for a walk-in cellar entrance.

On the grounds to the west are a stone dairy building and a frame smokehouse, where hams and sides of bacon hang from thick beams. A section of heavy brick wall with tall arched openings is the vine-grown ruin of an orangery—a family version of cointreau was one of the Mount Airy table products. Dressed stones protrude from the sod here and there, foundation fragments of long-forgotten out-buildings. The men's "necessary" was in this area, and one for the ladies was east of the house screened by a bamboo thicket. The only archeological exploration on the property so far is a 1945 dig of an outlying Indian burial ground. The area around the house, including a filled-in cistern, still holds whatever has been lost or discarded and received by the earth in all the Tayloe generations.

The dependencies were built before the house, and the family lived in the east building while the house was under construction. The west dependency, which housed the kitchen and servants' rooms, is across 150 feet or so of open ground. A frequent visitor during that period of dependency residence is said to have remarked that she never had eaten a hot meal at the Tayloes'.

The present owners of Mount Airy, Colonel and Mrs. Henry Gwynne Tayloe Jr., have installed a modern kitchen in the dependency passage. The colonial kitchen is still about as it must have been when last used—the iron cooking pots and implements appearing as though they had simply been put down at the big fireplace and not picked up again, in a kind of Pompeian state of interrupted activity. The intermediate kitchen, dating from the 1920s, is across the hall, with culinary artifacts of that period still in cupboards and on work surfaces. The sense of past time in a living continuum is forcefully present at this and other Virginia plantations. Out on the Mount Airy terrace a bowling ball was casually placed in the crotch of a yew tree after some long-ago game on the lawn. The tree, now a patriarch with branches sweeping the ground far out from a deeply ridged trunk, has imbedded the ball in thick wood growth.

At Mount Airy John Tayloe II achieved both a highly satisfactory dwelling and a landmark in American residential architecture. The fact that it was built of stone was in itself extraordinary, because stone was generally lacking in the Tidewater region, and stonecutters were rare indeed. By the mid-eighteenth century a few Virginia houses had been built with rubble walls, and some with front walls of ashlar (square-cut) stone set irregularly and with rubble walls at the rear and ends.

A fairly large deposit of hard gray sandstone was found on the Tayloe plantation, however, and it was quarried for the walls. Mount Airy, as Fiske Kimball wrote in 1922, was "perhaps the most ambitious house in the colony" in its use of ashlar courses in all the walls. The regularity of the courses is broken only here and there, and the dependencies reflect the same concern for an even, well-finished surface. Even the connecting passages are faced with squared stone, although in the forecourt walls the blocks are cut more painstakingly and have finer mortar lines than in the walls exposed to the side yards.

For the central pavilions—the prominent pedimented entranceways that frame doors and second-story windows on both sides—Tayloe got Aquia Creek sandstone, the same nearly white stone as that used a half-century later for the United States Capitol and the President's House—and in the Octagon. Aquia stone was used also for the window enframements, string courses (projecting horizontal bands), quoins (projecting dressed stones at the corners), and, at the top of the

18

John Tayloe I (1687–1747), the son of William
Tayloe, founder of the Mount Airy estate.
(Artist unknown).

*Smithsonian Institution*

terrace steps, for pedestals supporting a pair of big stone urns. From these steps
to those at the house entrance is a walk paved with red sandstone transferred
from the floor of the west connector when a new floor was laid there for the modern kitchen. The original source of this stone is not known.

The central pavilions were innovations of both craft and style. They show
a notable precision of cutting, fitting and rustication (deep mortar joints) of the
stone. They contribute to a baroque surface by their lighter color and their im-
posing compositions of subordinate forms, patterns and planes. The pavilions
are authoritatively contained within their facades and their architectural gram-
mar, which has much to do with the expressiveness of a grand style.

If there was an architect for Mount Airy, his identity has escaped the record.
The sophistication of the design urges that there must have been professional
involvement, and one candidate from very few possibilities would appear to be
John Ariss, who lived in the vicinity and whose name hovers about several houses
of that period by scholarly conjecture.

Ariss was a native Virginian who is believed to have studied architecture in
England. He is tentatively credited with having served as consultant to George
Washington in the remodeling of Mount Vernon, and with the design of Kenmore, the house built by Fielding Lewis, Washington's brother-in-law, at Fredericksburg. In 1751 Ariss advertised in the Maryland Gazette that he was capable
of designing "either in the Ancient or Modern Order of Gibbs Architect."

At that time several English books of architectural designs were circulating
in the colony. Among the most widely consulted were *A Book of Architecture* by
James Gibbs of London, and *Vitruvius Scoticus* by William Adam, a leading

19

Scotch architect who practiced early in the eighteenth century and was the father of the great Robert Adam. Master builders and amateur architects used plans directly from these books, often combining features of several plans with results that brought about innovative harmonies of mixed means, or turned out awkwardly, depending on the builder's capacity to adapt classical and baroque ideas to the limitations of labor skills and materials on remote estates.

The arcaded pavilion of Mount Airy's south facade is from a plate in Gibbs, derived from Andrea Palladio, the sixteenth century master, and the north facade is from Adam's book. William H. Pierson Jr. notes that Palladio's drawings are even in tone, but that Gibbs's subtle variations in hatching give coloristic effects that made the pavilion in the design adapted to Mount Airy seem lighter than the walls, "and the builder translated this pictorial suggestion of color literally by using two kinds of stone." He asserts that Mount Airy introduced a new colonial style, "the first authentic version of what can properly be called colonial 'Georgian' architecture."

Pierson points out that "Georgian" is more a dynastic than a stylistic term. The first three Georges reigned from 1714 to 1820, and a number of architectural styles are identified with that century. However, there is a historic American style —combining some of Sir Christopher Wren's baroque textures, some of Palladio's rational floor plans and facade compositions, some distant memories of Inigo Jones's classical precepts and some vagaries in the translation of all these by colonial builders—that is Georgian Colonial. For the Virginia gentry still firmly allied with England and its traditions, this manner was home away from home. As applied to colonial Virginia estates it proclaimed dominion over its land. The boldly defined chimneys, pediments, pilasters, quoins and window mullions, unified within a grand design, were emphatic elements of a manorial entity intended for a long succession of eldest sons.

Mount Airy is the first dated example in this country, says Kimball, of a broad center hall free of stairs, which were built in a corner room, thus liberating the hall for use as a sitting room of splendid amplitude. It was the first house in the colony to use curved walls to enclose the dependency connectors, and these wing-like features frame the forecourt space with a gracious dignity. Both the placement of stairs and the curved passages are from Palladio via Gibbs. This house was among the first to install the so-called Palladian window, a composition of central arched opening rising above rectangular side openings, which became a feature of later houses and public buildings, and is still popular. Two of these window compositions are centered in the east wall, one above the other.

In 1844 a maid carrying a candle on an errand to the attic started a fire that gutted Mount Airy. Mahogany paneling in the downstairs rooms was destroyed, and a heavy strong box bolted to the floor of a second-story room crashed through the marble first floor to the basement. The walls remained intact, and the interior was rebuilt. The stone chimneys were renewed in stuccoed brick, and the marble flooring was replaced with wood.

The interior doors were replaced from a property that the Tayloe estate

John Tayloe II (1721–1779), who built the present mansion at Mount Airy, in a portrait by John Wollaston. *Smithsonian Institution*

owned for some years in Washington—Fuller's City Hotel, which later became the famous Willard Hotel. Some fine six-panel doors were retrieved from a remodelling to take care of Mount Airy's losses. Those doors are still in place, with their brass hotel room numbers still attached.

The restoration work was done by George H. and William P. Van Ness, and while they were in the area they were called over to Blandfield, the William Beverley estate in Essex County, across the river. Blandfield, too, had fine paneling, but because it was recognized as a fire hazard following the Mount Airy disaster, Beverley had the Van Nesses take it out, giving rise to a local saying, "One house burned, two sets of paneling destroyed."

John Tayloe II grew tobacco, but his main interest was importing and breeding fine race horses. The plantation had its own race track, as did several others. The racing meets were big occasions that lasted several days and attracted visitors from long distances. The betting was heavy. Disputes sometimes drew blood at the track, and often ended up in court. The June and October fairs at Fredericksburg featured racing, with music, dancing, plays and sales of plantation products. A grand ball followed the races.

Philip Vickers Fithian, a student for the ministry from the College of New Jersey at Princeton, lived for a year at Nomini Hall, 12 miles west of Mount Airy, as tutor for the children of Councillor Robert Carter III, grandson of "King" Carter. Fithian was a guest at many plantation events in the Northern Neck, and his *Journal and Letters* is one of the best records of life in the country places. This is a glimpse of Mount Airy from Fithian's Journal of April 7, 1774, when he was invited to accompany Carter, one of his sons and two waiting men for an overnight visit:

> *Here is an elegant Seat!—The House is about the Size of Mr. Carters, built with Stone, & finished curiously, & ornamented with various paintings, & rich Pictures. This Gentleman owns Yorick, who won the prize of 500£ last November, from Dr. Floods Horse Gift—In the Dining-Room, besides many other fine Pieces, are twenty four of the most celebrated among the English Race-Horses, Drawn masterly, & set in elegant gilt Frames.— He has near the great House, two fine two story stone Houses, the one is used as a Kitchen, the other, for a nursery, & Lodging Rooms—He has also a large well formed, beautiful Garden, as fine in every Respect as any I have seen in Virginia. In it stands four large beautiful Marble Statues—From this House there is a good prospect of the River Rapahannock, which opposite here is about two miles across. We can also from the chambers easily see the Town Hobbes-Hole & the Ships which lie there. . . .*

Mount Airy, like other plantation manors, had many of the characteristics of a town. It was a community of workers and craftsmen engaged in the production of food, clothing, implements and luxury items for use on the plantation, and commodities for outside trade. It had monumental architecture in the great house, and vernacular design in the clusters of slave houses and in the barns, sheds and outbuildings. It had street circulation. There was easy access to a seaport, the town of Hobb's Hole, later renamed Tappahannock, across the river, where ships from many parts of the globe tied up. All sorts of goods—furniture, glass, dishes, bolts of fabric, madeira, farm animals and so on—could be ordered from Europe and delivered close to the plantation by the same ships that sailed away with the hogsheads of tobacco to satisfy the hearty English appetite for smoke and snuff.

The generations of Tayloes made good use of their land. Sir Augustus Foster, British minister to the United States before 1812, seems to have had a close enough friendship with John Tayloe III to know some details of his business affairs. Foster wrote in his *Jeffersonian America:*

> Mr. Tayloe had about 1,000 Negroes on all his estates of which he had some even in Kentucky and his lands being so scattered he had an overseer to each large farm . . . The wages of his white men cost him nearly £1,000 per annum in Virginia currency. The men and women appeared to take equal shares of work, but he treats them with great indulgence, and they seemed to like him . . . Mr. Tayloe might, I believe, be considered as the richest man in Virginia in 1806–7, being said to have then had $60,000 . . . per annum arising from 15,000 acres of land belonging to him in different parts of this state and Maryland . . . He was supposed to lay out every year $33,000 in purchasing land. . .

Some estimates put Tayloe's income at about $75,000 a year. Among other properties, he owned the Neabsco Iron Foundry established by his grandfather in 1734 on Neabsco Creek, then a navigable inlet off the Potomac River near Dumfries, about 20 miles south of Alexandria. There he had a house, made pig iron, built ships and sold flour and horses. In 1810 he became the proprietor of an agricultural and industrial venture on nearly 2,500 acres of land at Cloverdale, west of Lynchburg, that included another iron works. He built up holdings of business and residential property in Washington.

John Tayloe II had become a prominent turfman with such horses as *Yorick* and the mare *Selima,* the latter purchased from the estate of her importer, Benjamin Tasker Jr., of Annapolis, and still potent in the American Stud Book.

John Tayloe III enlarged on his father's reputation. He was the leader in American racing from 1791 until he became less active in 1806. His most famous horses included the mare *Castianira,* which he imported. She became the dam of *Sir Archy,* bred in partnership with Archibald Randolph, and *Sir Archy* sired *Lady Lightfoot,* one of the great mares of racing history. In 1798 Tayloe founded the race course in the City of Washington, and was president of the Jockey Club that operated it.

There is a family story about the club's first race, on November 6, 1798. A Washington tavernkeeper, name unrecorded, owned a horse named *Lamplighter,* which he wanted to race against Cincinnatus, owned by General Charles Ridgeley of Hampton, Maryland, and reputed to be the best runner in that state. The general sent word that "I accept challenges from gentlemen only." The tavernkeeper asked Tayloe to take over the horse and make the match. *Lamplighter,* running under the Tayloe colors, won the race.

Georgetown (*foreground*) and the City of Washington in the distance, looking southeast, about 1800. Drawn by G. Beck, and engraved by T. Cartwright, London. *Library of Congress*

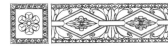 

# FOUR

# THE OCTAGON IS BUILT

ayloe's choice of a lot in the city of Washington in open country west of the partly built President's House was in accord with a strategy advocated by Pierre L'Enfant and concurred in by President Washington that it was important to establish nodes of development in outlying sections to stimulate fill-in growth. Most of the city's earliest private and commercial construction was south and east of the small first unit of the Capitol, in the areas where there would be quick business for hotels, taverns and boarding houses. City settlers interested in pioneering other parts were hard to find.

The Tayloe property was about a mile from Georgetown, which had been settled for a half-century, and it was about a half-mile northeast of a settlement called Hamburgh, which had been platted but only sparsely occupied in the area of the present Kennedy Center for the Performing Arts. Hamburgh was absorbed in the new city plan.

The only house in the near vicinity was a modest cottage down near the riverbank overlooking the Tiber outlet, the home of David Burnes, one of the 19 proprietors whose farms and plantations were taken for the new city. Burnes, an irascible Scotchman, had held out the longest against Washington's land-trading plan, and his boundary lines embraced some of the crucially necessary sites—much of the old Francis Pope holdings in the area of the future Mall and the President's House, as well as most of Pennsylvania Avenue. He had turned away the President's agent with harsh words, and held up the Pennsylvania Avenue surveying until he could cut his hay crop.

(Later Burnes was to mellow considerably when the profits from his land made him extremely rich. Soon after his death, his daughter and only heir, Marcia Burnes, was married to General John Peter Van Ness, a Congressman from New York and wealthy in his own right. He settled in Washington, and they commissioned a mansion by Benjamin Latrobe, who designed a severe Greek Revival exterior around regally luxurious rooms and appointments. The Van Ness mansion was completed in 1817, and until late in the century the old farmhouse of David Burnes still stood nearby. The mansion went through several ownerships, and went into decline after the Civil War, with its grounds rented for picnics. The Pan-American Building now stands on its site, but the Van Ness stable, also by Latrobe, remains in good condition at the corner of C and Eighteenth Streets.)

At the time of Andrew Ellicott's survey, 1792, Burnes was being treated with delicacy. For the time being the survey map left a tactful blank in the area of the cottage grounds—no square being drawn there and no number assigned.

Ellicott's precisely drawn survey shows 1,146 blocks, or squares, each one numbered. The term "square" was used with the utmost liberality, for the numbered land units produced by L'Enfant's scheme of grid and diagonal street patterns had the shapes of trapezoids, irregular pentagons, narrow and fat rectangles, geometric meanders, triangles, wedge-shaped slivers and sometimes squares. Square No. 1 was a triangle at Virginia Avenue and I Street, Northwest, now engulfed by freeway ramps, and No. 1,146 was a long rectangle at the end of East Capitol Street, on the Anacostia River.

Tayloe's lot was on the fourth square north of the Burnes cottage—Square 170, a long rectangle with its south side cut away on the bias by the diagonal of New York Avenue. Lot 8 was at the intersection of New York Avenue and Eighteenth Street, Northwest, which then had little if any preparation for service but were platted and named just as they are now. The diagonal cut-off gave the block an acute angle at this corner.

The first problem faced by William Thornton in preparing the architectural design was the same one that many a Washington architect has had to deal with since—to plan a house for an eccentric site, and to provide rational orientation with the streets. If the house were built to face either of the bordering streets, it would be at an ungainly angle in relation to the other street. Stables also had to be fitted in, with other outbuildings and two wells. Springs and wells were then the city's only water supply.

Although Thornton's lack of architectural training caused trouble in the practical aspects of some of his projects, his remarkable intuitions and his resourceful adaptation of architectural principles from the books that he devoured produced a number of buildings that stand out today as original and distinguished. His sense of style seemed to respond alertly from abundant imaginative resources to the challenge of difficult conditions, and it came through handsomely in the residence that the Tayloe family called the Octagon.

He dealt with orientation by relating the house equally to both streets, with identical side walls made parallel with New York Avenue on one side and with Eighteenth Street on the other. The corner is 70 degrees, and consequently these two walls are at that same angle from each other. A semicircular pavilion projects from the broad connecting front wall, and stone steps mount to a porch just large enough to shelter the doorway, which opens into a full-circle vestibule. The house is pulled back from the corner, leaving a small triangular planting space.

New York Avenue was not constructed to the full width provided for in the plat, and the difference leaves a yard next to the Octagon's south wall, which is on the building setback line. Consequently, a center line through the house would

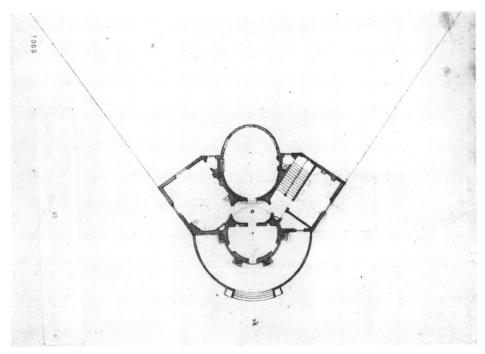

In preliminary study for the Octagon plan, Thornton sketched a large oval main room in the center, with stairway in what is now the drawing room.

*Library of Congress—Division of Prints & Photographs*

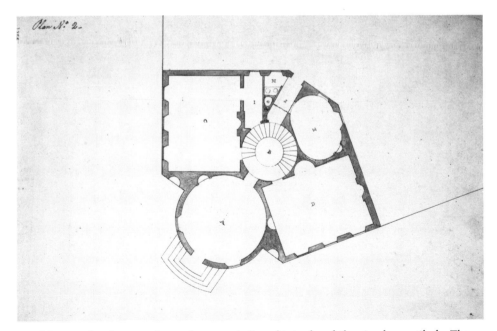

Second known sketch put staircase in center hall, and introduced the circular vestibule. The two main rooms are situated approximately as they were built.

*Library of Congress—Division of Prints & Photographs*

## TREATY OF GHENT ROOM

President Madison is believed to have ratified the Treaty of Ghent on the English rent table in the circular study on the Octagon's second floor. Table and some other furnishings are Tayloe originals. *Barrett.*

# DRAWING ROOM

The drawing room is furnished with fine examples of the period of John Tayloe III. Over the American Sheraton-style sofa is a Gilbert Stuart portrait of Mrs. William Thornton. A portrait of Thornton, the Octagon architect, also by Stuart, is over the chimneypiece. (Both portraits on loan from the National Gallery of Art). English Regency swan-neck mirrors flank the fireplace, over American Chippendale serpentine-front table. The English Regency chandelier dates from about 1810. *Barrett.*

Harkness 1888.

## VAN NESS MANSION

Benjamin Latrobe's Van Ness mansion, as it appeared from the Octagon, is shown in this
1888 watercolor by A. Harkness, with the Smithsonian Institution building at left and
the newly completed Washington Monument, then the world's tallest man-made structure,
also visible. *Barrett/Government Services Savings & Loan Association*

## DINING ROOM

Paint layers found behind an added partition showed the dining room colors to have been a soft green and off-white, to which it was restored. Hepplewhite dining table and chairs, the mahogany sideboard and a Scots breakfront (not visible) were gifts. *Barrett.*

## WINE CELLAR

Kegs of wine were stored in vaulted brick cells in a half-circle basement room beneath the vestibule. Removal of a concrete floor slab revealed herringbone brick, gouged from the impacts of dropped kegs. *Barrett.*

## BASEMENT KITCHEN

Before the big basement kitchen fireplace are arranged the dishes of a Christmas dinner such as the Tayloes might have served in their early years in the Octagon. *Washington Star photo*

## AMITY BUTTON

The "amity button," a little disk of ivory or metal set in the stairway newel post, signified that the house was satisfactorily built and was paid for. The Octagon has a pair of newel posts, each with its button. *Barrett.*

strike the Eighteenth Street curb a short distance north of the street intersection, instead of bisecting the corner angle. This fortuitous off-axis placement of the house contributes a graceful effect of having avoided being plugged into this acute angle and impaled on its own geometry.

The only right-angled corners in the exterior plan are the turns from the flared-out side walls to short rear walls—the fireplace ends of the principal rooms on each floor. The broad main chimneys are imbedded in the windowless planar surfaces of these walls, through which they pass with no outside indication of their existence until they break through the cornice. There is one more wall, connecting the chimney walls across the back yard; in it are cut the main rear entrance, a separate door to the servants' stairway, a centered Palladian window (lighting the main stairway) and seven other windows, above a basement areaway. This sixth side completes the circuit, for in fact the Octagon is not octagonal. Evidently the front pavilion got confused long ago with two more sides, and as far as the Tayloes were concerned the house was the Octagon; so it remains.

At either side of the rotunda-like entrance vestibule, in semicircular plaster niches, are small black iron stoves crowned by very large urns, believed to date from the Octagon's beginning. The vestibule floor is paved with squares of gray and white marble, laid diagonally. Ahead is the arched doorway to the stair hall.

The six-panelled front door swells outward in a gentle curve that continues the curve of the wall. The two closet doors of the vestibule also are curved with the wall, and so are the three doors in each of the circular rooms above it on the second and third floors. So are the doors in the first and second floor stair hall that open into the service stairway, and two doors flanking the rear entrance. One can imagine the consternation that such a specification would cause today: 13 panelled doors made to swell ever so slightly to fit curved walls. The service stair doors and a flat one from the dining room into a closet were made with panels, but to maintain symmetry with the opposite walls the panels were filled flush with plaster and painted like the walls. Their hardware is visible, but they are exceedingly understated, and disguised to the extent that chair rails and base moldings are continued across the doors and are precisely mitered to make the joints unnoticeable when the doors are closed.

Opening off the stair hall on the right is the drawing room, with three tall windows overlooking New York Avenue across the side yard; the dining room is in a counterpart arrangement on the left, overlooking Eighteenth Street at closer range. These rooms are behind the splayed side walls, and the same composition is repeated in the upper stories with variations of room layout.

The Octagon's inner spaces are arranged with such clarity that there is only momentary consciousness of shifts in axis from one side to the other, and no feeling that the flanks are marching to different drummers. Past the circular vestibule and within the winglike diagonals the rooms are familiarly regular in form, and the perception of the stair hall as a rectangular space is little qualified by its rounded corners in the stairwell and its other corners slightly skewed for the walls of the circular rooms.

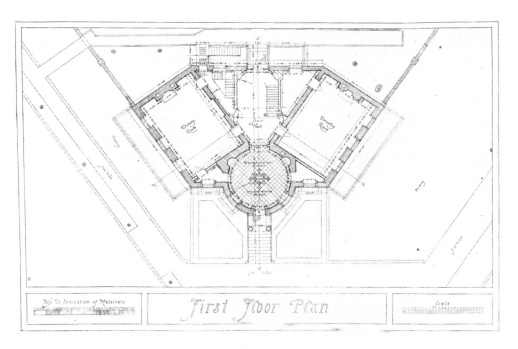

*First Floor Plan*

In the large triangular space between the splayed-out drawing and dining rooms was built the main stairway, with the service stairway partitioned off at left. The similar space adjoining the drawing room is believed to have been Tayloe's office. *Brown*

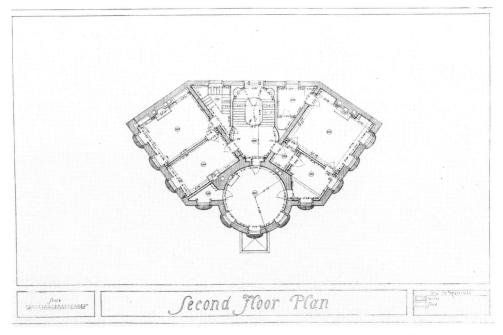

*Second Floor Plan*

Second-floor plan shows the thick wall structure, with extra chimney mass in the circular wall. Fireplaces on each floor, plus the vestibule stoves, required 16 flues in all. The present main gallery space was made by removing partition between the two bedrooms at left. The graceful contours of 11 iron balconies can be seen outside the windows. *Brown*

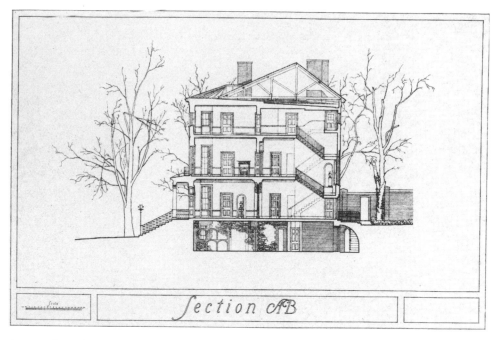

*Section AB*

Section through center of the Octagon, from front to back, shows the wine vault cells, main stairway and the original flat roof slope under the added hip roof. *Brown*

The floor plan, however, shows what inventiveness went into the congenial arrangements and the provisions for easy, efficient movement. In the Octagon plan Thornton combined three basic geometrical forms—the circle (pavilion), the rectangle (side wings) and the triangle. The stair hall, minus the walls that enclose the stairway, is an isosceles triangle with its unequal side the rear entrance wall. This triangle, the basic central structure but perceivable only in the plan, is so large that its partitioning with parallel walls for the stairwell still left commodious behind-the-scenes spaces, both right triangles, at the base corners of the big central triangle. A servants' stairway zigzags from basement to third floor in this enclosure on the dining room side. The outside servants' entrance is on the first floor landing, and there is a door into the dining room from this passage, so that the table could be served from the basement kitchen by private access.

The counterpart spaces beyond the stairwell partition on the other side had various household uses—a dressing room off the second-floor master bedroom, probably storage in the third-floor space.

The use of the space thus gained on the drawing room side of the first floor was puzzling, and it was usually referred to as a pantry although it is on the other side of the hall from the dining room, and in the drawing room circulation area. (It is indeed now used as a pantry and small kitchen for serving receptions in the second-floor galleries.)

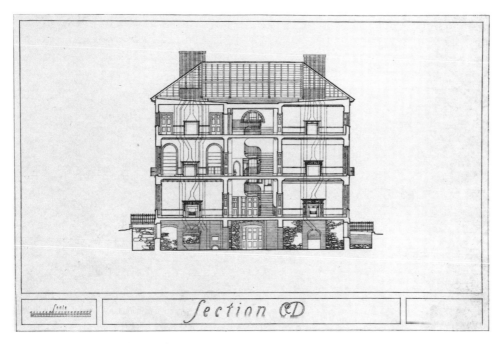

Center section from side to side shows flue patterns of the two rear chimneys. *Left:* The basement kitchen, dining room above it, then two bedrooms. *Right:* Basement servants' room, drawing room above it, then the Dolley Madison Room and third-floor bedroom—now the curator's office. *Brown*

What seems to have been a more obvious and necessary use in the early years of the Octagon occurred to two Lynchburg architects and historians, J. Everette Fauber Jr., and Robert H. Garbee, who did extensive research on the house for the American Institute of Architects Foundation in connection with the most recent restoration. Tayloe's study was the second-floor circular room above the vestibule, now called the Treaty Room because of the historical event that later occurred there. But Tayloe could hardly have wanted the traffic of his numerous business visitors and workmen upstairs in the private family quarters, and would seem to have preferred for his office in town a room—this large triangular room—more convenient to the rear center hall entrance and well apart from space that Mrs. Tayloe might have been using to receive the callers who were constantly a part of the Washington social pattern. Supporting evidence was found when probing of the wall exposed a large arched recess, similar to the one where the sideboard stands in the dining room. It appeared that the recess was originally planned for the inside wall of the drawing room, but that it was changed to become a feature of the other side of this wall in the anteroom—evidence that this space had a higher degree of finish and more exposure to visitors than it would have had as a servants' facility.

An innovative feature of the Octagon for its time was the closets, on every floor and tucked into more of the triangular spaces at junctures of the larger building units. They were left-over spaces, circumstances of the Octagon's unconventional configuration, the kind of spaces that in many a house would have been sealed off and forgotten. Thornton used every one, and their generous capacity and convenience must have well served the family with its numerous children, and often with cousins from Maryland and other relatives and friends occupying the second and third floors.

Another Octagon puzzle is the famous "tunnel"—a brick-vaulted underground chamber adjoining the basement kitchen, with at least four feet of masonry between them. It is entered from the north end of the basement areaway, and extends on the same grade as the areaway floor along the outside of the kitchen wall 27 feet to the corner of the house nearest Eighteenth Street. It is about 6 feet wide.

A popular supposition is that Tayloe had a tunnel built to the river bank for the delivery of supplies, but it is hard to make sense of this. A brick tunnel of that size with vaulted ceiling all the way to the river, then about a quarter-mile, would have been costly in money and effort out of proportion to its doubtful advantages. Its construction would have depleted the Mount Airy work force, and would have taken many thousands of bricks in a brick-hungry new town. It would have had to run beneath Eighteenth Street or across private property, either way involving complicated easements, and it would have had to surface on or near the precincts of the testy David Burnes. Since the Tayloes were accustomed to a much longer over-the-road haul between Mount Airy and their Rappahannock River landing, it seems improbable that they would feel the need of a private subway in Washington.

Fauber has suggested that the vault could have been a cistern, with a circular opening found at the top admitting the sucker-pipe of a hand pump, or that it might have been a root cellar, with the opening as a vent. Later he found evidence of a well of "fine water" beneath the kitchen, which argues against the cistern. Garbee proposes that the vault was a coal bin, and that the legendary tunnel to the river could have been a drain constructed of brick, probably serving the Octagon and other properties as the area was built up. He and fellow researchers found drains under the basement floor that had been connected with the downspouts of the Octagon's original flat roof. They ran southward, toward the river. Time ran out on this investigation because of the required completion schedule, and the drains were covered up. Picking up other systems along the way, these could have needed an outlet big enough for a small boy to crawl into, and small-boy memories could have exaggerated the drain into a tunnel.

There are substantial gaps in the history of the Octagon, and historians had become resigned to the possibility that family records relating to its construction were destroyed in the 1844 fire at Mount Airy. Recently, however, the Virginia Historical Society completed cataloguing previously unknown Tayloe family papers, found in trunks and chests that had been stored in the east dependency at Mount Airy, and some in a window seat. The papers include the account books of John Tayloe III and record copies of his letters. Garbee went to Mount Airy for an afternoon of searching for Octagon material in these, and remained for two days.

Later, Colonel and Mrs. Henry Gwynne Tayloe Jr. graciously parted with a large number of the papers for deposit with the Historical Society.

Besides their immense value to students of Virginia and American history, the papers shed considerable light on details of the Octagon's construction and its completion date, which is usually given as 1800. The new evidence indicates that major construction was done by then, but that the house was not ready to be lived in until late in 1801. It also shows that the house cost more than double the $13,000 figure mentioned by Thornton in his note to George Washington.

In "An examination of the houses in the city of Washington," made in November, 1801, and recorded in *Site and Building Records for Federal City*, Vol. 1799, is the report:

> In Square 170: Houses completed
> prior to May 15, 1800 None recorded.
> Houses completed since May 15, 1800
> Brick 3, Wood three.
> Houses to be completed by Nov. 15
> 1801 None listed.

The Tayloe house does seem to have helped encourage the building of others in that area. The Octagon apparently was one of the three brick houses, and this notation seems to support the 1800 completion date.

Perhaps a clearer distinction is necessary between "completed" and "finished" in the dating of architecture, between the structure all put together and the interior made ready for occupancy. There can be quite a time lapse between these conditions. (Building contracts today often use the term "substantially completed"—the point when the contractor's work is finished except for corrections.)

Two entries in the diary of Mrs. William Thornton, wife of the architect, have been taken as evidence of the 1800 date. On January 7, 1800, she wrote: "After dinner we walked to take a look at Mr. Tayloe's house, which begins to make a handsome appearance." That suggests a fairly well advanced construction stage. On the following November 27 she wrote that "Dr. Thornton came at one o'clock for us to go see the chimney pieces at Mr. Tayloe's house," and this indicated that the house was nearly finished if she meant the mantels for the drawing room and the dining room, because they were to be made of delicately wrought English Coade stone,* and would be among the last installations.

---

*Coade stone is a kind of fine-grained terra cotta, putty colored, of a secret formula that has been lost. Its invention has been credited to a Richard Holt who patented it in England about 1772. The business was taken over by Mrs. Eleanor Coade, apparently Holt's daughter, and was carried on by her daughter, also named Eleanor Coade. The factory at Lambeth engaged first-rate artists, and its products were widely used in England as architectural sculpture and ornament, mural reliefs and table tombs. "In many a weather-worn facade, the Coade sculptures stand out crisp and firm," wrote Sir John Summerson in *Georgian London*, "and I have seen burned churches where the Coade monuments are the only ones still recognizable." Most of the Coade wares are signed "E. & W. Coade" or "Coade and Seely." The firm seems to have stopped production about 1836.

From third story to brick-floored basement, the service stairway makes a spectacular zigzag.
*Mel Chamowitz*

However, if the Tayloes expected to see the Coade chimney pieces on this visit they were disappointed for some letters in the new-found papers reveal Tayloe irritatedly trying to get delivery of these mantels, and of the bases and capitals of the same material for the two front porch columns—which did not come from London until the summer of 1801. A letter of June 14, 1801, reflects concern about completion time, and chronicles troubles with deliveries of furniture and materials, an unsatisfactory workman and unexpectedly high expenses. The letter was addressed to William Lovering at Georgetown, evidently Tayloe's superintendent:

*Sir:*

I was in hopes to have heard fully from you by yesterday's Post, & I have to beg you on the receipt of this write me fully what has been done since I was up—& what still remains to be done; & the soonest Period; when you think the House—stables & inclosures of the Lott can be fully compleated, I am in daily expectancy of my furniture, & wish the House compleated with all speed to receive it particularly as I wish to inhabit it early this Fall—the drawing Room & dining room had best be left to the

Iron-grilled entrance to the "tunnel" is in the rear basement areaway. The underground vault, probably a coal bin, now houses part of the air-conditioning system.  *Chamowitz*

last to finish—on acct on the Chimney Peices, because we must substitute a finish, if the missing Peices are not found all the Rest of the House, can be proceeded on with all possible dispatch—In the course of a Month I hope to be with you, when most of the work I expect to see done; the sooner you get the Furniture from Webb for the room I wished finished & furnished for my use the Better—if McDaniel does not conduct himself properly—I wish you wd consult Mr. Dorsey—for in this case t'would be well to discharge him from all future interference with the house, and to measure up his work— & be done with Him—in which case you could employ such Workmen—as are fit to make a finish and carry on the Business without any fuss—for I recollect you told me McDaniel was of no use—The man employed about the staircase with some good workmen with him wd— with yr care & attention do it as well—if not better than McDaniel—hav$^g$ any further to say ab$^t$ the Work—Please consult Mr. Dorsey & act for the best—my Object is to be done with the Building as Quickly as I can— with the least Trouble & Vexation—for the Expence of it already alarms me to Death, whenever I think of it

Your obed$^t$ Serv$^t$

14th June 1801    John Tayloe

("The room I wished finished & furnished for my use" may have been either the second-floor study or the conjectural first-floor office.)

A letter of July 16, 1801, to "Messrs. Lamb & Younger, Merch$^{ts}$ London," complains about the service from Coade:

In the packages of Chimney Pieces, the principal one—the mantle of the drawing room Chimney Piece . . . is intirely missing—therefore unless the Piece be immediately sent so as to be put up before the room is finished Coades Bill ought not to be paid, without a deduction for this Piece, which is the principal one of the whole—the Portico Pieces if not already shipt, I wish now to be paid no farther attention to—for the Building can't wait for them—please forw$^d$ my letter to Coade.

An 1801 record, with no further date, is an itemization of materials paid for:

Payments for bricks, nails, sand, glass ($528.35), plank, hair, mahoghany, glue & oil, lime, furniture from B'more, marble, paper, chairs, hair cloth, hire of mason, bell hanger ($150), 2 girders for stable, 140 cords of wood

and this is followed by a list of the persons paid. It concludes: "Total, 1799 through 1801—$28,476.82."

The Decatur House, completed in 1818 on the President's Square (later Lafayette Square), cost much less than that if its estimates were reasonably accurate. Its architect, Benjamin Latrobe, wrote to Stephen Decatur, his client, that he believed the estimates from two builders were between $10,000 and

$11,000, with fencing, stabling or pavement to be another $1,500 to $1,800, and not counting papering and the three principal chimney pieces. (Remembering that Thornton had vastly underestimated the Tayloe house one is inclined to consider the Decatur estimates open-ended.) Fauber found that the Monroe house at 2017 I Street, N.W. had been sold in 1808, soon after its completion, for $10,000. Both of these were among the city's finest residences.

In December, 1801, Tayloe recorded an invoice for "354 yds 2 coats Plast'ring, 342½ straight stucco, 388 feet Sup. of Plain Cornice." (Stucco was the ceiling plaster, with ornamental work.) There were other entries for "run of frieze, astragal & ribbon, nich and 2 nich heads, soffits, architrave, enrichments, beads." These undoubtedly were installations already made at that time.

Summary invoices covering work apparently done in 1801 and 1802 are for "Leveling Area walls, Fitting Compossition Chimney pieces (the Coade mantels), Balconys Digging and laing foundations to Steps Cutting holes fixing palasades and Chimney Pots," and for brick paving, walls, gutters and drains, painting and gold leaf work in the drawing room and "101 feet Ionic Dentil Cornice etc." among other joiners' work.

The notation of a payment of March 24, 1803, includes the sort of items that signify occupancy:

Plaistering, putting hay in loft, deepening two wells, supplies, including
1 Bbl Cyder, cash paid Lucy for meat & Bread, 2 lb candles & 1 qt Whiskey

The mention of hay in the loft and previous references to the stables indicate that this construction was approximately concurrent with that of the house, thus settling another long-standing question. There are two other records of special interest:

1801 Dec. 24 unto 31 To the brick-work at Setting up
    Four Coal Fire-grates at 2 Doll$^s$ P. Grate
1802 To Brick-work at Setting up
    One Coal Fire-Grate

Tayloe was buying large quantities of firewood, 140 cords being mentioned in the 1801 itemization, but he was quickly converting at least some fireplaces to coal. Garbee suspects the source of coal to be the old Huguenot workings near Richmond, an available and likely source. That would mean shipment by boat in fairly large quantities, with ample storage needed near the house and out of sight, all of which strengthens the case for the tunnel space as a coal bin. It would be interesting to know whether the coal grates or any other of the considerable iron work in the Octagon was produced by Tayloe's own Neabsco foundry, but no evidence has been found either for or against this possibility.

In December, 1800, the time for the transfer of government from Philadelphia to the new City of Washington, the Capitol was a small, hastily built three-story building that is now a part of the Senate wing. The President's House was the unfinished shell in which Abigail Adams was using the audience room for hanging laundry, and was having trouble getting enough firewood delivered to keep some of the rooms decently warm. Plaster was still setting and paint still drying in some areas, and in others both were yet to be applied; the main stairway was not yet built.

Two other government buildings had been erected, one for the Treasury Department, designed by George Hadfield, just east of the President's House and approximately parallel with its south facade, and a duplicate building for the Executive and War Department in a corresponding site on the west.

When the government moved in, Washington was still as raw as any frontier town. Pennsylvania Avenue was a precisely surveyed line of mudholes. As one of its first acts in Washington, Congress voted $10,000 for a sidewalk on the north side of the street. This was made by spreading chips from the sandstone blocks being cut for the Capitol construction. Makeshift as the sidewalks were with the sharp chips and their residue of dust or mud according to season, they were better than the street, which was subject to floods from Tiber Creek and was not surfaced until the 1830s.

The increased rate of construction attracted some of the country's best architects, among them Benjamin Latrobe, English-born and trained as both architect and engineer. He came to this country in 1796, its first fully professional architect, by modern standards. Latrobe and the self-trained Thornton were frequently rivals.

Tayloe seems to have consulted Latrobe about a plan for his house. In his biography of Latrobe, Talbot Hamlin notes that the architect had put a picture of a house on the title page of a proposed book of designs, with the inscription "Mr. Tayloe's house in the Foederal City." The title page is dated September 8, 1799, and Fauber points out that by then the building would have been under construction as Thornton's project. He notes, too, that the Latrobe plan is for a larger and more expensive house on a square-cornered lot, with a stable on axis with the house—which would not fit Lot 8. This suggests that the plan may have been drawn as a proposal before Tayloe bought his irregular lot, and it is even conceivable that it may have been initiated when Tayloe was thinking of a house in Philadelphia, where Latrobe was then based, and relabeled. Hamlin speculates that Tayloe may have favored Thornton because his political views were more in harmony with Tayloe's Federalist convictions. Moreover, Thornton's residence in Washington would assure closer contact once the Tayloes had decided on that location.

Thornton's construction plans for the Octagon have not been found, but two preliminary studies indicate the development of the scheme. In what seems to be the earlier study, the main room is a large oval on axis with the entrance and projecting into a rear bay. What is now the drawing room was subordinated, and its space includes the stairway. In the other sketch, the stairway is circular and at the center of the house. The vestibule has assumed its circular shape, the oval room is diminished in importance (it finally disappeared), and the two major rooms are entered from the front of the stair hall, as in the final design. There is no second stairway in either of these studies, and Fauber suggests that the private service stairs may have been prompted by Latrobe's design, which included them.

Like Latrobe, Thornton was attentive to his client's need of an ample stable to house his fine horses and equipages. The stable drawings show concern for making this building a worthy architectural complement to the house, and he gave it a prominent central element with arched openings (a feature that added to the enjoyment of the reading room during the years after the stable had been converted to the AIA library with these openings as generous windows). The alignment of the stable's east wall with the obtuse angle of Lot 8 showed that it was built prior to 1806, the year in which Tayloe purchased Lot 7.

The Admiral Storer house in Portsmouth, N.H., remarkably similar to the Octagon, was demolished in 1880, and the little that is known about it now is summed up in a photograph that is Plate 101 in John Mead Howells' *Lost Examples of Colonial Architecture*. Its rounded front projection looks shallower than the segment of a circle, and its side walls have two windows on each floor, as compared with the Octagon's three. A front porch with upper balustrade extends completely across the front wall. The house sits tightly and symmetrically within its corner. This house has been tentatively ascribed to Charles Bulfinch, whose family had Storer connections. Its relationship to the Octagon— as source idea, derivation or remarkable coincidence—is enigmatic.

Thornton deserves more thorough study. He was born on the island of Tortola, in the West Indies, May 20, 1759. He was reared in England, studied medicine in Edinburgh, and received his degree at Aberdeen in 1784. He did further study in Paris, and traveled widely in Europe. In 1790, soon after coming to the United States, he was married to the English-born daughter of Mrs. Ann Brodeau, who conducted a fashionable school for young ladies at Philadelphia. After brief residence on Tortola, the Thorntons moved to Washington in 1794, where they had a house at 1331 F Street, N.W. Thornton spent the rest of his life in Washington. They had no children.

Thornton had a wide range of interests, but the active practice of medicine seems to have been the least of them. Benjamin Ogle Tayloe, son of John Tayloe III, wrote in his *Memoirs* that "He had a well-earned reputation for letters and taste; he was a wit, a painter, and a poet." But Thornton was no dilettante. He wrote papers on a variety of specialized subjects: astronomy, philosophy, finance, government, art, language and medicine, and some of his contributions to these disciplines were innovative.

He was associated with John Fitch in steamboat experiments on the Delaware River, before Robert Fulton on the Hudson—another source of friction with Latrobe, who had invested in Fulton's venture. Thornton was granted patents for several steam devices. He invented a process for converting sawdust into planks, similar to today's particle board, and a repeating rifle, among other things. At the time of the War of 1812, he was Superintendent of Patents.

47

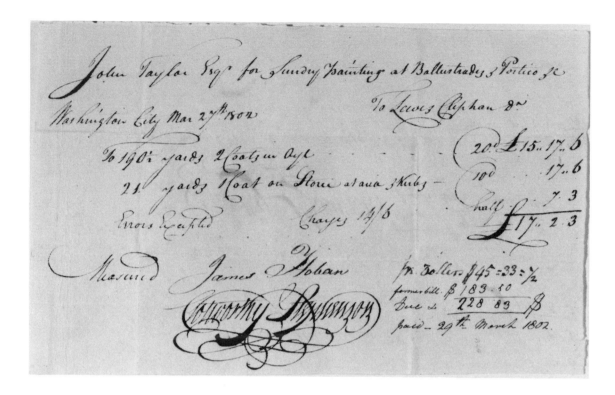

Invoice dated March 27, 1802, "For Sundry painting at Ballustrades & Portico" of the Octagon is signed by James Hoban, architect of the President's House and supervisor of construction of the Capitol, as city measurer. *Virginia Historical Society.*

The Capitol design competition was announced in this advertisement of March 14, 1792, in newspapers of Washington and other cities. *Maryland Historical Society*

**WASHINGTON,** *in the Territory of* **COLUMBIA.**

## A PREMIUM

Of a LOT, in the City, to be defig-nated by impartial Judges, and FIVE HUNDRED DOLLARS, or a MEDAL of that Value, at the Option of the Party, will be given by the Commiffioners of the Federal Buildings, to the Perfon who, before the Fifteenth Day of July, 1792, fhall pro-duce to them the moft approved PLAN, if adopted by them, for a CAPITOL, to be erected in this City; and TWO HUN-DRED and FIFTY DOLLARS, or a MEDAL, for the Plan deemed next in merit to the one they fhall adopt. The Build-ing to be of Brick, and to contain the following Apartments, to wit:

A Conference-Room,  sufficient to ac-
A Room for the Repre-  commodate 300
fentatives,  Perfons each.  Thefe Rooms
A Lobby or Antichamber to the latter,  to be of full
A Senate-Room of 1200 fquare Feet Area,  Elevation.
An Antichamber or Lobby to the laft.

Twelve Rooms of 600 fquare Feet Area each, for Committee-Rooms, and Clerks' Offices, to be of Half the Elevation of the former.

Drawings will be expected of the Ground-Plats, Elevations of each Front, and Sections through the Building, in fuch Directions as may be neceffary to explain the internal Structure; and an Eftimate of the cubic Feet of Brick-Work compofing the whole Mafs of the Walls.

*March* 14, 1792.  THE COMMISSIONERS.

# FIVE

# THE BEGINNINGS OF
# AMERICAN PROFESSIONAL
# ARCHITECTURE

A t certain stages of all construction jobs in the City of Washington, a city agent, called a measurer, would be called in to certify that so many feet of stone had been laid, plastering applied, balustrades painted and so on as the basis for payment The name signed to the invoice as measurer for painting of the Octagon balustrades and portico, and the base ment area and curbs, was James Hoban. The James Hoban who held this routine position was at the same time the architect who had designed the President's House and was then supervising its construction; moreover, he had been for several years the superintendent of construction at the Capitol.

The Capitol, as previously noted, was designed by William Thornton, who had little experience in construction work. The commissioners wanted a full-time superintendent of construction, and offered this position to Thornton, who declined. The important function of seeing that construction proceeds according to plans and specifications, now automatically a part of the architect's respon-sibility, was then subject to separate arrangement.

In 1800, when the Octagon was nearly completed, Thornton was serving as a member of the District Commission and, although not directly supervising the Capitol construction, was closely following its erratic progress. Thornton was making drawings for the landscaping of the President's House grounds, which he sent to the Secretary of the Navy. This seems not to have been carried out. At that time, too, another house with which Thornton has been identified was about to be built—Woodlawn, near Mount Vernon, given by George Washing-ton to Nelly Custis and his nephew, Lawrence Lewis, after their marriage. Mrs. Thornton's diary states that "Dr. T. has given him a plan for his house," but it is not known whether the house as constructed followed his plan. (Woodlawn now is owned by the National Trust for Historic Preservation.)

With the Octagon architect's time and attention spread over so many activities, it is not surprising to find his client, John Tayloe, involved in con-struction decisions, ordering and paying for materials, and encountering serious cost over-runs. We find the Thorntons going to the house in November to see

One of Thornton's studies for Tudor Place in Georgetown. With further revisions, the mansion was completed in 1816. *American Institute of Architects*

chimney pieces that Thornton, as architect, should have known were not even delivered yet. And it was Tayloe, rather than his architect, who pursued this matter through the London dealers until the next summer.

The loose relationship of the American architect with his projects in those days had become increasingly evident and troublesome as the pace of construction was being stepped up in the rapidly growing cities, and as projects got bigger and more technical. In the post-colonial period, the architect's qualifications and responsibilities were not defined by any generally applied standards. There were no examinations, no licensing provisions, not one school of architecture in the United States.

The term "architect" was applied with little discrimination both to master builders who could translate sketchy plans into finished buildings, and to cultivated men who became interested in building design as a personal devotion and could afford the time for studying it. The gentlemen architects—Thomas Jefferson is an outstanding example—planned their own houses, and some got into fairly extensive architectural practice by assisting their friends and finally accepting commissions. The best of them were serious students and observant travelers. With the books then available both the gentleman architect and the master carpenter could create buildings of high quality. They were guided, too, by well-established stylistic and construction traditions. It was their adaptation of whatever lore and skill they possessed to the conditions of their own localities that advanced the American building art in the only way that it could be advanced at that time and under those circumstances.

It was in this context of what may seem now to be provincial innocence that the competitions for the design of the Capitol and the President's House were conducted. The competitions were not necessarily a great turning point in the elevation of American architecture to a professional discipline, but they brought

William Thornton's front elevation of the Capitol, drawn at Tortola, with an optional choice for wing design on panel at right. It was a considerably revised plan (now lost) that he submitted to the Commissioners. *American Institute of Architects*

into clearer focus some of the shortcomings of architectural procedures of that time, and the newly found Octagon records echo this distinctly on the residential level.

It had been considered that Pierre Charles L'Enfant, the planner of the Federal City, also might design the Capitol and the President's House. L'Enfant, trained in Paris as an artist, volunteered in the American Army of the Revolution in 1777, illustrated Baron Von Steuben's manual of *Regulations, Order and Discipline for the Army of the United States*, and met Washington at Valley Forge, where he drew portraits of him and other officers. The indications are that his art training was extensive enough to have included study of architecture and of the great examples of civic design afforded by the gardens of Versailles and sections of the city of Paris itself; at any rate, in New York he practiced as an architect, did considerable residential work and remodeled the city hall as the first capitol of the United States. When he heard that a new federal city was to be planned, he wrote to Washington to offer his services, and was accepted.

After L'Enfant was relieved of his position, for refusing to follow instructions of the District Commission, the commissionners determined to hold competitions for the Capitol and the President's House. The competitions were advertised by posters in Washington in March, 1792, and in newspapers throughout the country in April through July, calling for submissions by July 15 —an unrealistic time limit. The President's House competition was won by James Hoban, trained in Ireland as artisan and architect, who came to the United States shortly after the Revolution. He practiced in South Carolina, where he designed the Statehouse that was burned in the Civil War. His competition prize was $500 and a gold medal, with employment at 300 guineas a year to supervise construction.

The Capitol competition was more complicated. It attracted at least 14

"East View of the Capitol," an elevation by Stephen Hallet that he sought, as supervisor of construction, to impose on the accepted design by William Thornton. *Maryland Historical Society.*

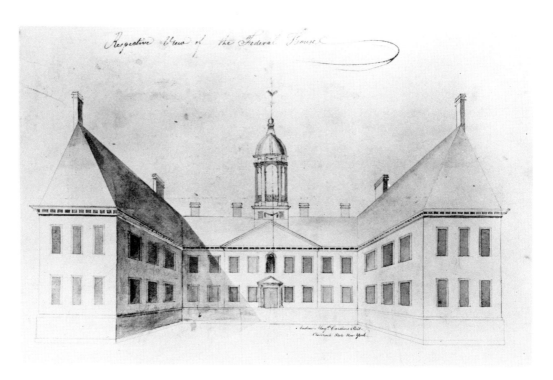

The only Capitol competitor who attempted to represent his design in perspective was Andrew Mayfield Carshore. His "Respective [sic] View of the Federal House" is the first recorded use of this technique in an architectural drawing in the United States. *Maryland Historical Society.*

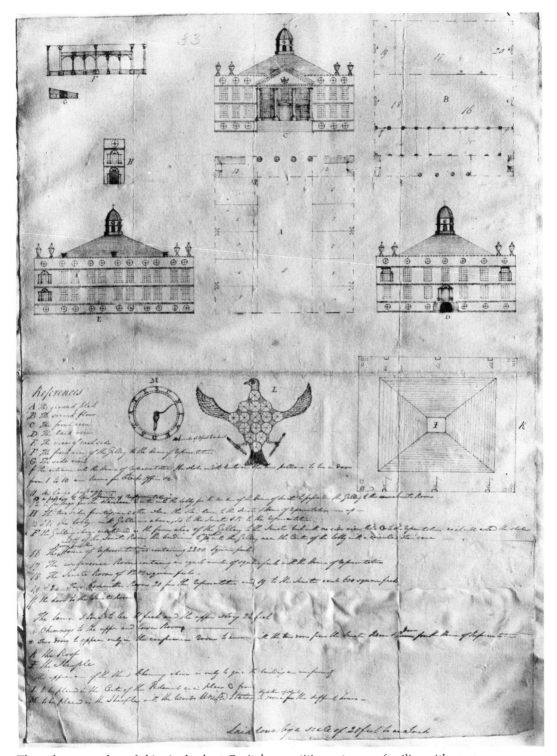

The unknown author of this single-sheet Capitol competition entry was familiar with some architectural terminology. His front facade resembles L'Enfant's Federal Hall, New York City, but his rear elevation has a droll disarray of windows. The eagle was intended for the front pediment. *Maryland Historical Society.*

entries, derived from pattern books or from observation of European buildings and classical models, as was the design for the President's House. Some of the submissions displayed a high degree of assimilation of these ideas, but a prevalent difficulty was with the control of scale in fitting together large elements and subordinate details in this unprecedented American monumental design problem. An otherwise creditable scheme by James Diamond, of Somerset County, Maryland, was given the unfortunate distraction of a colossal weathercock: an eagle taller than the main entrance and nearly as tall as the dome. With some reluctance, the commissioners determined that a design by Etienne Sulpice (Stephen) Hallet, who also had come over from France, was promising enough to justify further development, which they asked him to come to Washington to carry out.

It was at this point of indecision that Thornton wrote from Tortola in July, 1792, asking permission to submit a design. Permission was granted, and he took his studies with him in October to Philadelphia, from where he again wrote to the commissioners. He delivered his design the next January, and it was approved, in Washington's words, for its "Grandeur, Simplicity and Convenience."

James Hoban was prepared by training and experience to supervise the construction of his President's House, and his main problem was to get funds from Congress to keep the work going. The Capitol, however, was beset by a new array of difficulties. With Thornton unable to supervise construction, the commissioners engaged Hoban to supervise the Capitol, as well as the President's House. Then, as consolation to Hallet for depriving him of the prize, they gave him the job of studying the Thornton plans to make cost estimates, and in addition appointed him as draftsman and assistant supervisor under Hoban. Even though this did not then strike anyone as a breach of ethics, it should have been apparent that it was a case of bad judgment. Because Hoban was needed nearly full time at the President's House, Hallet was actually in charge at the Capitol. He made a number of unauthorized changes in Thornton's plans; some were necessary adjustments, but some deviations on which he actually began construction reflected his resentment at losing the competition. Hallet was fired, and Thornton—from the power base of his position on the District Commission —to which Washington appointed him in 1794—gained authority over the new supervisor, George Hadfield, who served and resigned twice by 1798. Then Hoban again was put in charge.

Because of this succession of fumbles only a small unit of the Capitol was ready to receive Congress on that first Monday in December, 1800. It was to shelter both houses, the Supreme Court, the Circuit Court and the Library of Congress for several years.

It was not until Benjamin Latrobe was appointed Surveyor of Public Buildings and Architect of the Capitol by President Jefferson in 1803 that an architect with such extensive professional training and outlook had official standing in Washington. Latrobe had an engineering degree from a German university, and had completed an architectural apprenticeship in England under Samuel Pepys Cockerell, architect and surveyor to the East India Company. Latrobe planned the Tiber Creek Canal locks, and designed the naval drydock on the Anacostia River, the first in the New World. He rebuilt the Capitol from the burned ruins of 1814, but his work was confined largely to the interior.

A higher and more explicit standard of professional qualifications pervaded American architecture after Latrobe, but the practice of atelier training under an established architect was to continue for a long time. The development of the architect with full authority over the plan, the specifications and the construction was resisted by the clientele, who could see no reason to put the architect in charge of what had traditionally been done by the builder (or undertaker, as he was known then), and it was resisted by the builders, who did not welcome intrusion on their time-honored authority. Widespread recognition of the architect's professional role had to wait for the need to assert itself, which it did as construction became more technical, budgets more restrictive, building codes more legalistic, the need for coordinating many operations more imperative, and industrial technology more prevalent.

The American Institute of Architects was founded in 1857 to establish a high level of professionalism in architecture, and to achieve recognition of its standards. But it was 1866 before the first independent course in architecture was offered anywhere in the United States, at the Massachusetts Institute of Technology, followed by the University of Illinois in 1870 and Cornell in 1871, all as adjuncts of engineering schools. It was not until 1890 that an architectural school was established in the context of fine arts, at Harvard.

The Capitol and President's House competitions emphasized the distance that the architectural profession still had to travel to establish discipline and competence in the large conceptions of urban design and construction, and the distance that clients still had to go in understanding the need for responsible design and supervision. Events in the new City of Washington laid the groundwork for both.

Thornton was at his best in the role of gentleman architect, as demonstrated in the individuality of two great houses that he created—Tudor Place in Georgetown and the Octagon. It can only be conjectured what he might have done if he had concentrated on architecture or, for that matter, on any of his numerous talents.

President James Madison, a copy of a portrait
by Gilbert Stuart, ca. 1800(?) Loan, Penn.
*Academy of Fine Arts, Philadelphia.*

# SIX

# FROM PRESIDENT'S HOUSE
# TO SLUM DWELLING

I t is evident that the Tayloe house was far from finished in time for the social activities accompanying the transfer of the federal government to Washington in December, 1800. It seems a fair presumption, though, that some of the family would have made a path through the building materials, and would have had servants put a room or two in temporary order and build fires. That was what President Adams and the first lady were doing in their clammy mansion, and it was the kind of camping that must have been going on in other partly finished houses in the new capital. A good many wives of Congressmen and other officials postponed going to Washington until the city could be made more habitable, but they were to find that that would take years.

A half-century later the Tiber Creek Canal was an open sewer, fed by drains along its bank. By the 1850s L'Enfant's far-extended street system was still largely unpaved, except for some token gravel. Pennsylvania Avenue was macadamized in 1832, and cobblestoned in the late 1840s. Pigs still roamed the streets during the Grant administration.

But in 1800 Washington had its United States Theatre, with reasonably regular performances; it had Samuel Harrison Smith's newspaper, the *National Intelligencer and Washington Advertiser*, and it had the publisher's wife, Margaret Bayard Smith, who found Washington pleasant and stimulating, and who set a civilizing example by making light of discomforts and cheerfully enjoying the city's abundant activities, to which she called attention in voluminous letters and published writings. A housing inventory that year reported 109 brick dwellings and 263 built of wood, the latter erected under an easing of the building code to encourage construction. The population was 3,210, including slaves.

Builders' sheds and material yards nearly surrounded the President's House, and construction workers had a shanty town at Hamburgh. The President's House faced Samuel Davidson's brickyard and kilns in the area of the present Lafayette Square. Davidson supplied brick for the President's House, the Capitol, the Octagon and many another building.

In their journeys from Mount Airy to Washington the Tayloes had options of transport by either water or land. The most persuasive possibility, in the absence of known description, is that wagons carrying baggage, provisions and servants would have been sent on ahead a few days early to open the Octagon, unpack, get the kitchen fires going and warm up the big beehive oven. Perhaps there was a resident overseer, who would have seen to it that there was hay in the stable and fuel for the fires, and would have kept the grounds in good order.

The family members could have traveled in a coach or two with, one imagines, Tayloe and his older sons on horseback. Or Tayloe might have ridden in a curricle, a two-wheeled chaise drawn by a pair of horses, such as the one that Sir Augustus Foster's memoirs recalled as the conveyance in which he and Tayloe once made a visit to Neabsco.

Not far from Mount Airy was "King" Carter's road to Fredericksburg, about 60 miles away. From there to Alexandria was another 50 miles or so on the King's Highway, the Williamsburg road along an old Indian route, the Potomac Trail—approximately today's State Route 1 and Interstate 95. Dumfries, where Tayloe had his Neabsco Iron Foundry and a house for use when he visited his works, was midway between Fredericksburg and Alexandria. The plantations of hospitable friends were all along the way as possible overnight stops, those nearest to the city being Mount Vernon and Woodlawn. A ferry was available for crossing the Potomac to one of the Washington landings or to Georgetown. By 1809 they could cross the Potomac via Long Bridge, at Fourteenth Street.

Traveling at carriage speed of eight or nine miles an hour, the journey could have been made in two days without unusual effort. It was not uncommon for travelers to have horses kept along frequently used routes for fresh motive power. An English officer who toured the colonies in 1764 and 1765 wrote that the Virginians traveled "frequently Sixty Miles to dinner . . . you may conclude from this their roads are extremely good."

Once the Octagon was ready for regular use, which Fauber's document research indicates was by November 15, 1801, the family seems to have occupied it mainly during the winter season for the remainder of Colonel Tayloe's lifetime. Here the record yearns for an impressionable journal-keeper or letter-writer. Its first 10 years are disappointingly undescribed, but there are notations that it was the scene of many a bountifully served gathering of capital personages and visitors. The first child to be born in the Octagon was Edward Thornton Tayloe, in 1803. Six other children of this family were born there.

Tayloe's account books refer to work done and things delivered to "house in city"—wood and coal hauled, a brick wall repaired, a pump mended, $2 paid to a chimney sweep—but the family seems to have regarded its town house as a natural concomitant of its level of existence. The Octagon was used to the best advantage and managed well, but taken in stride. In 1806 Tayloe bought Lot 7, adjoining his Lot 8 on the east, and there are indications that an outside kitchen and servants' quarters were in outbuildings there.

The year 1815 was the Octagon's date with world history. Following two

A British conception of the burning of Washington, showing well-groomed British officers directing the destruction of public buildings by their smartly uniformed troops, on August 24 and 25, 1814. The illustration is from an English history. *Library of Congress.*

years of give and take battle action in the War of 1812, the British sailed up Chesapeake Bay and, on the evening of Wednesday, August 24, 1814, marched into Washington. Within a few hours the Capitol, the President's House and other government buildings were in flames. President Madison had left two days before to be with his militia. Dolley Madison escaped in a carriage just ahead of the invasion with as much as she could carry—documents, silver plate and a few personal things, after having hastily broken the frame of the Gilbert Stuart portrait of George Washington and turned the canvas over to two men who were assisting her. Her steward, Jean Pierre Sioussat, known as French John, took her parrot in its cage over to the residence of the French minister, Louis Serurier, for safekeeping by his chef.

The residence of the French minister was the Octagon.

August was not the time of year when the Tayloes normally used their town house, but there are differing accounts of where they were and of how the French minister happened to be staying at the Octagon, and of the sequence of events when it seemed that enemy troops were about to destroy the city. In the ghastly shock and disorder hardly anybody was taking notes—except for Dolley between trips to the roof to watch the approaching British through her spyglass. Otherwise, the civilian experience of the capital city invasion is recorded in fragmentary reports that open little peepholes into the scene, and in vignettes of dramatic confrontations.

After rain put out the British fires, the President's House remained a masonry shell. It was reopened with a New Year's reception by President and Mrs. Monroe in 1818.

On the night that the British were setting fires, Serurier sent a messenger to General Robert Ross, who was presiding over the destruction of the President's House (the Capitol having been gutted by marines under Rear Admiral Sir George Cockburn), and asked that the Octagon be spared, since it was the French embassy. Ross replied that the house would be "as respected as if His Majesty were there in person; and that he would give appropriate orders." (The British did little damage to private property.)

Benjamin Ogle Tayloe, the oldest son in the Octagon family, whose *Memoirs* are generally accurate but whose recollections of the 1814 episode were set down some years afterward, wrote:

> *Prior to the British invasion of Washington, Colonel Tayloe, though a Federalist and wholly out of sympathy with the war party, nevertheless was in command of the cavalry of the district.*
>
> *Superseded by an officer of the regular army, he was sent to Virginia to bring up some of its militia in season to aid in the defence of the Capital. His efforts proved ineffectual, and he was returning home, when he met my mother on the road, making her way to his place, Neabsco, near Dumfries, in Virginia. She had vacated the Octagon, and induced Mons. Serrurier, the French minister, to occupy it, with a view to its protection.*

Serurier's account of his protective action gives the impression that he had been living at the Octagon for some time.

The Patent Office and the Post Office were temporarily housed in what had been Blodget's Hotel on the north side of E Street, between Seventh and Eighth,

Northwest. This was another of Thornton's domains, for after the District Commission was dissolved in 1802 he was appointed clerk, then Superintendent, of the Patent Office. When he heard that the British were destroying government buildings, he hurried to the Patent Office accompanied by a Mr. Nicholson, "my model maker and messenger." As he described the incident in a report written a week later, George Hadfield and a man named Lyon were already at the scene. A British major, unnamed, was in charge of a detail of soldiers. The major said that private property might be saved.

"I told him," Thornton wrote, "that there was nothing but private property of any consequence, and that I was willing to have any other burnt in the street provided the Building might be preserved which contained hundreds of models of the Arts and that it would be impossible to remove them; and to burn what would be useful to all mankind would be as barbarous as formerly to burn the Alexandrian Library for which the Turks have been ever since condemned by all enlightened nations. The major desired me to call again to Col. Jones . . . I went and was kindly received. They took their men away, and promised to spare the building." This was the only government building not destroyed by the British.

A violent storm of wind and rain sent the British back to their ships. The windstorm did considerable private property damage—and so did looters—but the rain put out the fires. Thornton's intervention had saved a building in which Congress could meet, but the President and his wife, returned from a rendezvous at the home of friends near Langley, Virginia, had no residence. They took shelter at the home of Richard Cutts, the Thornton's next-door neighbor at 1333-35 F Street, who was Dolley Madison's brother-in-law.

Several circumstances combined felicitously to make the Octagon the first temporary official residence of an American President. The French Minister was about to move to Philadelphia, and Benjamin Ogle Tayloe wrote that his father had sent a courier from Mount Airy to offer the use of his house to President Madison. At the same time, Thornton was suggesting this to the Madisons as a possibility, and it also occurred to Serurier, who had referred to the Octagon as "the best house of the city." Serurier wrote:

> Seeing, that by the burning down of his mansion, the President was without a suitable dwelling, I made him an offer of my house. He excused himself at first, but in such a fashion as to make me insist, and he finally accepted it expressing to me how sensible he was of my consideration.

With Thornton undoubtedly helping to make arrangements, the Madisons settled in the Octagon September 8, 1814, for occupancy until the following March. The Presidential office was set up in the circular study on the second floor. Dolley Madison replenished her wardrobe with a new array of Paris gowns, and re-established Washington social life in the Octagon drawing room with a succession of receptions and parties. For New Year's Day, 1815, she reserved an ensemble of particular splendor—a robe of rose-colored satin with ermine trim, gold chains around her waist and arms, and as headdress a white satin turban with a tiara of white ostrich plumes.

The treaty that ended the War of 1812 had been signed at Ghent, Belgium, on December 24, 1814. It still remained, however, for the treaty to be approved by the United States Senate and ratified by the President. It was the next February 17 when Henry Carroll, who had been on the American staff at Ghent, delivered the document to the Octagon in a small leather-bound casket. President Madison signed it, from all indications, at the circular mahogany table that is now in the room.

The solemn ceremony of the signature was followed by a welkin-ringing party, beyond question the biggest of many big social events at the Octagon. Drinks were ordered for all the servants, and Paul Jennings, the President's valet, said afterward that French John was drunk for two days. Joseph Gale Jr., co-owner of the *Intelligencer* who covered the celebration, wrote:

> *Soon after nightfall, Members of Congress and others . . . presented*
> *themselves at the President's house, the doors of which stood open. When*
> *the writer entered the drawing room . . . it was crowded to its full capacity,*
> *Mrs. Madison (the President being with the Cabinet) doing the honours*
> *of the occasion. And what a happy scene it was. Among the members*
> *present were gentlemen of opposite politics, but lately arrayed against one*
> *another in continual conflict and fierce debate, now with elated spirits*
> *thanking God, and with softened hearts cordially felicitating with one*
> *another upon the joyful intelligence . . . But the most conspicuous object in*
> *the room was Mrs. Madison herself, then in the meridian of life and*
> *queenly beauty . . .*

Later the Madisons moved to a smaller house at Pennsylvania Avenue and Nineteenth Street. James Hoban went back to work on the ruins of the President's House, but President Madison and Dolley never occupied it again. It was the newly elected President and Mrs. James Monroe who opened the rebuilt mansion, with new French furniture, on January 1, 1818. White paint covered the scorched exterior stone, and the mansion, which had been casually referred to as the White House before the fire, now became generally identified by that name.

When the Tayloes reoccupied their house, it began to be used increasingly for year-around living by various members of this amicable family, who came and went for the next 37 years. Colonel Tayloe stayed out of politics, and his guests represented diverse convictions. B.O. Tayloe wrote that his father "maintained until his death an establishment renowned throughout the country. Here he entertained in the most general manner, all persons of distinction, whether Americans or foreigners, who visited Washington, and imparted an elevated tone to society in that city."

The only structural change made by Tayloe in the Octagon was the addition of a hip roof that was first shingled, later covered with terne (tinned sheet steel),

Dolley Madison, as portrayed
by Wood, ca. 1814.
*Virginia Historical Society*

then shingled again. It was built with its ridge near the rear wall, above the original flat roof. This may have been done in the summer of 1818, when Tayloe's records show payment of $4,750 to "Mess'rs. Early and Homan, Building Contractors," for unspecified charges made in April, June and July, a favorable time for roof work. An 1813 water color of the house shows it crowned by a parapet, and one painted between 1830 and 1840 shows the present roof form.

Thornton strongly preferred flat roofs because they were out of sight and because he considered them better for drainage. In response to questions by Latrobe about the Capitol roof, Thornton wrote January 1, 1805:

> *It is next to impossible to put any elevated covering that shall resist the ingress of water when the gutters are filled with snow . . . I proposed a flat roof made with a composition that has since been found to answer perfectly . . .*

And after the burning of the White House, he wrote to Jefferson:

> *I also should recommend an alteration in the roof of the Pres. House. It looks much handsomer now, in ruins, than before the destruction. The roof was very heavy, Hoban being a carpenter, made very heavy roofs.*

Thornton's "composition" on the Octagon roof was canvas laid over heavy battened boards and impregnated with bitumen, with a gentle slope to a gutter at the rear wall, concealed behind the parapet and drained by two downspouts. Jefferson also preferred the flat roof, and built it at Monticello and the University of Virginia. They leaked and so, evidently, did the Octagon. The new roof, designed by George Hadfield, was built over heavy trusses and framing, with decisive slopes and with gutters completely around the building—a structure that was complicated by the Octagon plan.

Where Samuel Davidson's brickyard had been, Lafayette Square began to take form. L'Enfant had designed this green as part of the President's grounds, but at Jefferson's urging during his Presidency (1801–09) the land was returned to the district. The first building on the square was St. John's Church, at Sixteenth and H streets, straight north of the White House. It was completed in 1816 from a design by Benjamin Latrobe, who also was its first organist, and was enlarged later by James Renwick and other architects. Tayloe, said his son, "was the largest contributor" to this building, and to St. John's he presented "the massive church service of silver which formerly belonged to the old church of Lunenberg in Richmond County, Virginia," and which had been sold at public auction under a court decree in 1813.

In 1818 Latrobe also designed for Commodore Stephen Decatur the first residence to be built on the square, on the northwest corner. It is now the headquarters of the National Trust for Historic Preservation. The Richard Cutts House (successor to his house on F Street), later owned by the Madisons, was built in 1820, facing the Decatur House across the square, thus anchoring the square's two north corners. The Blair House, around the southwest corner on Pennsylvania Avenue, went up between 1824 and 1827, and then came the house that Benjamin Ogle Tayloe commissioned for himself in 1828, near the Cutts-Madison House. With the high quality of Lafayette Square established, other distinguished houses followed to make this one of the country's great urban ensembles.

Benjamin Ogle Tayloe was married in November, 1824, to Julia Dickinson of Troy, New York. They lived in the Octagon until 1829, then moved to the Lafayette Square House, which he had leased out for a year after its completion. For 30 years this was his observation post on the Washington political and social scene, and the place where he wrote the penetrating and often biting comments of his *Memoirs*.

John Tayloe III died February 29, 1828, at the age of 57, and was buried in the family cemetery at Mount Airy.

William Thornton died a month later, on March 28. He was buried in the Congressional Cemetery, overlooking the Anacostia River, where Senators and Representatives who died in Washington were for some years interred under identical monuments—ponderous sandstone cubes that sit on the graves with a dark finality, the stones that Senator Hoar of Massachusetts complained added a new terror to death. Thornton was accorded the honor of being admitted to the Congressional ranks, beneath one of these monuments, all made from a design of his principal rival, Benjamin Latrobe.

Tayloe's will provided that, if necessary to pay his debts, the family sell

> ... my house and lots in the City of Washington (including my dwelling
> house after the death of my wife). The furniture at my said dwelling house
> after my wife's death, except the plate ...

A sale wasn't necessary, and Mrs. Tayloe continued to live in the house, with various daughters and sons-in-law.

The Octagon has accumulated an abundance of ghost stories, one of them acknowledged by the family. The family story was written by Virginia Tayloe Lewis, Tayloe's granddaughter, who was born in 1843 at the Octagon, 15 years after his death. Her account is in a manuscript titled "Washington Society Before the War."

> The bells rang for a long time after my Grandfather Tayloe's death, and
> every one said that the house was haunted; the wires were cut and
> still they rang ... Our dining-room servant would come upstairs in the
> evening to ask if anyone rang the bell, and no one had.

She was referring to the servants' call bells, which hung in the basement and were connected by wires to pulls in various rooms of the house. (The bells and pulls were lost in later years, and restorers of the Octagon supposed that the system of wires had been dismantled. When moldings were removed during structural repairs, however, the wires were found concealed in races under the moldings—another of Thornton's ingenious devisings. They are still in place.)

Other ghost stories are much more spectacular, and there are persistent legends that two unspecified daughters of Colonel Tayloe fell to their deaths from the third-floor stairway landing to the first floor—a spot where visitors (never identified) have been said to feel sudden chilly drafts. Then there is the slave girl story in two versions: (a) killed by a British soldier, who concealed her body in a hollow wall (to appreciate the precise knowledge he would need of the wall structure to find a hollow space, see floor plans, Chapter IV), or who (b) took the stairwell plunge to escape an ardent British naval officer, who then leaped after her, fatally.

There are reports of the chandelier swinging unaccountably, foot tracks in third-floor dust, cooking aromas from the museum kitchen, and unexplained sounds. Two phenomena were reported by identified witnesses—a physician visiting the caretaker's wife said he encountered a man in dress of about 1800 on the stairway, and a later caretaker in 1963 twice found the Octagon lights on and the doors open after he had closed the house for the night and departed—and he had the only key. Hans Holzer reports in his book *The Ghosts That Walk in Washington* that he visited the Octagon in 1969 (while restoration was in progress) with a medium, who in a trance heard the name "Alice" called out, and associated the name "Mary" with the body of a woman being carried out of the house on a stretcher.

Both the Tayloe girls are supposed to have had disagreements with their father over marriage plans. One account has it that the eldest daughter loved a

Did one, perhaps two, Tayloe girls fall to their deaths in this stairwell? Legends of ghostly visitations say yes, but family records say a firm no. *Barrett.*

British officer, to whom her father had forbidden the house because of anti-British feeling. After a loud argument on the stairway, she stomped to the top floor with her candle; there was a scream, and her body plunged down the stairwell. A flickering light is still to be seen on the stairway on stormy nights, according to this story, with sounds of shrieks and sickening thuds.

The other girl is said either to have eloped or was considering marriage to a man beneath her station: another argument on the stairs, another tumble and another ghost.

With no inclination to dematerialize any good ghost story, it must be pointed out that all the Tayloe daughters can be accounted for, and that none of them fits any of the stairway legends. Two of them did predecease their father—Rebecca, who died at the age of 18 at Mount Airy, and Anne, who died in infancy. There was no "Alice" among them, and in fact with all their numerous large families and their need for many girls' names, the Tayloes seem not to have used this one. In his genealogy, W. Randolph Tayloe does not list any Alice either in the family or in its marriage connections until 1933. The nearest to "Mary" among the daughters of John Tayloe III is the middle name of Elizabeth Merry Tayloe—for the British minister of 1803–06, Anthony Merry, a friend of her father. Elizabeth was born in 1806 and married in 1829, the year after her father's death; she died in 1832, on her twenty-sixth birthday, leaving two children. Her death occurred in Washington, perhaps at the Octagon. (For the full roster of the Tayloes' eight sons and seven daughters, see Appendix.)

The youngest daughter, Anne Ogle Tayloe, and Henry Howell Lewis were the parents of Virginia Tayloe Lewis, author of the manuscript that mentions the ringing of the call bells. They lived at the Octagon until after the death of Mrs. John Tayloe. Their daughter's christening celebration, February 26, 1843, was attended by members of the diplomatic corps, and little Virginia was toasted by the Secretary of the Navy. She was intimately a part of Octagon life through her impressionable childhood years.

Miss Lewis spent the latter part of her life with a nephew and his family at Baltimore, and was the great aunt of a little girl of this family who was her namesake and now is Mrs. René Maurice Stéphan of Columbia, South Carolina. Miss Lewis preserved family records, now in Mrs. Stéphan's care, had a good memory and loved to tell stories about her life at the Octagon—none of which included references to ghosts or mysterious happenings.

Miss Lewis's manuscript makes one other passing reference in this context following the death of Mrs. Tayloe in the summer of 1855, "esteemed as the last survivor of the ladies of the old school in Washington," as one account put it. Soon afterward the family's occupancy of the Octagon came to an end, although its ownership continued. Virginia Tayloe Lewis wrote:

> Soon after my dear old grandmother, Mrs. Tayloe, died, in her 83rd. year, we left 'The Octagon.' It belonged to the two eldest sons, and all the silver, according to English law, went also to the sons ... The breakup at 'The Octagon' was very sad, but, as I was a child, I enjoyed the change and was glad to get away from the haunted house and its ghostlike marble statues which often frightened me.

The marble statues were in tall niches on the first stairway landing. It has not been determined when the house began to be called the Octagon. No mention of it by that name was found in Colonel Tayloe's records. The first such reference in other family papers found so far is in a letter to Benjamin Ogle Tayloe from his brother, Edward Thornton Tayloe, of March 1, 1837, with the postscript, "Our love to Mother & Anne & Nancy Ogle who are all, I suppose at The Octagon—they never favor us with a line." The offhandedness of this reference suggests that the term was in prevalent use by the family.

Following Mrs. Tayloe's death, there seems to have been a misunderstanding among the sons and daughters about the disposition of the house, then occupied by the Lewises and other daughters. In a "Memo About Octagon Plate," in the Tayloe Family Papers at the University of Virginia Library, B. O. Tayloe wrote:

> About the Octagon the ladies refused to accept my repeated offers to them & those since made by W.H.T. at the Virg'a Springs—They rented another house—& after I had rented The Octagon I only heard elsewhere they wished to continue at The Octagon—never from them. They were only duly notified by me of having a tenant engaged and when he was to take possession.

"W.H.T." was the next-oldest son, William Henry Tayloe. In the English tradition of property rights that was adhered to by many Virginia families, keeping the family silver in the male line of descent was as firmly adhered to as was the tradition of primogeniture in land. Even so, to make amends to his sisters, B.O. Tayloe offered them several items of silver *"needed* for their *use."* This apparently was worked out.

The tenant to whom B.O. Tayloe referred is not identified, but he seems to have responded to this notice in the *Daily National Intelligencer* March 10, 1856:

> 'For Sale or Rent' The House corner of New York Avenue, and 18th.
> Street, commonly called 'The Octagon'. For terms apply Joseph C. Willard,
> Willard's Hotel.
>
> Benj. Ogle Tayloe<br>William H. Tayloe

Among Tayloe's commercial town properties, the one that became the best known was the predecessor of the famous Willard Hotel. Tayloe owned several lots at the northwest corner of Pennsylvania Avenue and Fourteenth Street. In 1816 he built a row of two-story houses with attics along the Pennsylvania Avenue frontage. The corner house was leased for hotel use, and the others were later all made part of the hotel. The establishment went under several names, but it attained its first prominence as Fuller's City Hotel.

Many notable visitors stayed at Fuller's, including Charles Dickens on the 1842 tour that produced his pungent *American Notes*. Washington proved not to be the author's favorite city, and the hotel as he described it was not the magnificent hostelry that it became in later years:

> *The hotel in which we live is a long row of small houses fronting on the street, and opening at the back upon a common yard, in which hangs a great triangle. Whenever a servant is wanted, somebody beats on this triangle from one stroke up to seven, according to the number of the house in which his presence is required; and as all the servants are always being wanted, and none of them ever come, this enlivening engine is in full performance the whole day through. Clothes are drying in this same yard; female slaves, with cotton handkerchiefs twisted round their heads, are running to and fro on the hotel business; black waiters cross and recross with dishes in their hands; two great dogs are playing upon a mound of loose bricks in the centre of the little square; a pig is turning up his stomach to the sun, and grunting "That's comfortable!" and neither the men, nor the women, nor the dogs, nor the pig, nor any created creature, takes the smallest notice of the triangle, which is tingling madly all the time.*

After Tayloe's death, the hotel property was supervised by B.O. Tayloe. On a business trip to Troy, New York, he took the steamboat *Niagara* up the Hudson River from New York City, and met Henry A. Willard, the steward who attracted business to the boat by resourceful attentions to the passengers' comfort. Tayloe invited Willard to manage what was then known as the City Hotel. Willard took over the management in 1847 under a lease, and was joined by his two brothers, Edwin D. and Joseph C. Willard. They changed the name to Willard's City Hotel, and in 1853 purchased the row of houses, which the Tayloe estate had expanded to 40 rooms, consolidating them into one four-story building. In one of these remodelings, the interior doors became available for the rebuilt Mount Airy. Within a few years there was a new six-story building, and this was replaced in 1901 by the present Willard Hotel building designed by Henry J. Hardenbergh. There were two later additions. The hotel was closed in 1968, and its future is in litigation. It was placed on the National Register of Historic Places in 1974.

On August 22, 1856, B.O. Tayloe bought out W.H. Tayloe's half-interest in the Tayloe properties in Washington, including the Octagon and its two lots, for $15,954. W.H. Tayloe inherited Mount Airy. At the time of Mrs. Tayloe's death the neighborhood had deteriorated, and so had the house. In 1860 the Octagon was leased to the Rev. Charles White, pastor of St. Matthews, for use by St. Rose's Technical Institute, a girls' school, with an agreement that Tayloe "repair such plaster as may have fallen, such roofs as require it, sash chords where they have failed, windows where broken, and restore such woodwork as may have become decayed."

Some Tayloe furnishings had remained in the house, as indicated in a deed that Tayloe drew up in 1864 offering the property to the church for $20,000 "excepting only certain articles of furniture as understood between the parties, especially statues and mirrors." The sale did not occur. It is not known what became of the marble sculptures.

From 1866 to 1879 the house was rented by the government for the Hydrographic Office. B.O. Tayloe died in 1868, leaving all his Washington property, except his house on Lafayette Square, to his daughters with the curious condition "that none of them live in Washington."

The Octagon received little maintenance after that; its rooms, and even attic space, were rented to a hodgepodge of commercial and residential tenants. Glenn Brown, secretary of the American Institute of Architects, visited the house in 1886 to make drawings of it for the *American Architect*, Boston, and found it "almost squalid."

Although the family had stopped maintenance, it still felt solicitude for the house. Brown was asked by Mrs. Leland Stanford, wife of the Senator from California, to purchase the drawing room mantel "without placing a limit on the price." Mrs. Stanford wanted it for temporary use in Washington, and then for her California home. "I found that no monetary consideration would induce the heirs to mutilate the property," Brown wrote.

On his next visit, in 1898, he found the Octagon occupied by eight or ten families, the mantels masses of dirt, rubbish piled four to six feet high in the drawing room, and stove pipes cut into the chimney flues above the rubbish-filled fireplaces.

A thick growth of vines had climbed the front walls, but the Octagon's exterior was in generally good condition when the American Institute of Architects rented the house in 1898.

*Frances Benjamin Johnston / Library of Congress*

# THE OCTAGON RESTORED

T he course of the Octagon toward ruin, and the direction of the American Institute of Architects, then in New York, toward a Washington headquarters began to converge in 1896. At the thirtieth convention of the AIA the executive committee was empowered to arrange for facilities in the capital. The next year the committee, with Glenn Brown as a member, reported on several possibilities, and recommended:

*It is thought more desirable for the Institute to have its own building; the 'Octagon House,' one of the best examples of work done in the year 1800, can be secured for thirty dollars a month; its plan, character of design and workmanship, and location make it peculiarly suitable for the headquarters . . .*

The committee was authorized to negotiate a five-year lease at a rental of no more than $360 a year, and to issue up to $5,000 in debentures to pay for repairs. The house and grounds were being managed by a trust company, and the terms were that the Institute would put the house in order and maintain it, with the option of buying it at whatever figure the owners might be offered by any other party that would induce them to sell, and that in case of sale other than to the Institute, the AIA would be reimbursed for its repairs. The lease was signed and repairs begun in the fall of 1898. On January 1, 1899, the American Institute of Architects moved into the Octagon.

The AIA was eager to own the house, and as the lease approached its fifth year the president, Charles Follen McKim, authorized Brown to offer $30,000 for the building, one-third in cash. Brown had to tell McKim that the Institute had just $500 in its treasury. McKim said he would ask for contributions, but would personally guarantee the cash payment. The offer was accepted, and the Institute found itself in possession of "22,322 square feet of ground, being 174 feet on New York Avenue, and 181 feet on 18th Street; containing dwelling, stable, and smoke-house."

There is a full-circle fulfillment in the fact that the 1902 deferred payment notes that benefited the Octagon in its hour of need were signed by McKim and

71

When the Octagon restoration was begun, the back yard was shaggy with weeds and neglected trees. An added rear door enclosure was sagging. A small window had been cut into the wall next to the third-story window at right; it was removed in restoration.

*Johnston / Library of Congress*

Brown as AIA trustees in a private room of the White House, for which the Octagon was a fortuitous substitute 88 years earlier. President Theodore Roosevelt was not present, and probably was unaware of this obliquely significant event. It simply happened that McKim, Mead and White were then reconstructing the White House interior, with Brown as their superintendent; they were conveniently together on those premises, and it seemed rather bully to carry out that bit of Octagon business there. To make the coincidence even more arresting, the Presidential family was again living in a borrowed house, this time at 736 Jackson Place, on the west side of Lafayette Square.

Given a cleaning and basic repairs, the Octagon immediately attracted offers to lease and one for purchase at $50,000. The Institute declined all offers, and began an analysis of the building's condition as the first step of a restoration program.

In 1902 historic preservation was by no means an idea whose time had come. The outstanding precedent was the perseverance of the Mount Vernon Ladies' Association of the Union, founded in 1853, to save George Washington's house from physical collapse and public indifference. The early efforts at preservation were largely causes taken up by women's organizations, and the public was inclined to view such activities as genteel hobbies.

The term "adaptive reuse" was still more than a half-century in the future, but this conception of keeping a landmark building in existence by restoring it to serve a new purpose consistent with its historic character was exactly what the AIA was working toward in a voluminous sequence of reports and resolutions.

It is unlikely that any preservation project ever had the attention or the participation of more architects. The Institute had committed itself to a building that was important on a number of points—because of its role as a vote of confidence in the new capital, its service as the Presidential residence in an emergency, its having been the scene of the ratification of the Treaty of Ghent, its social and political panorama of notable people who had been welcomed there, and its long association with a prominent family.

These memorable associations were high qualifications in themselves for the restoration, and reasons of this kind remained the most persuasive and the easiest to justify in preservation issues long afterward. The Octagon, however, had another qualification: it was an excellent example, and one of the earliest, of a landmark advancement of independent American building design. The restoration itself has bestowed another chevron on the Octagon, as the first American building to become the focus of a major preservation effort in which architectural importance was paramount.

All buildings exist in the context of the traditions and teachings of other architecture, and every building says something, incidentally or intentionally, about its own culture. The power of a building to communicate ideas—about its structure, its form, its materials, its ornament, its identification, its situation with relationship to other buildings, its usefulness and its moment in time is summed

When the American Institute of Architects rented the Octagon in 1898, it engaged Frances Benjamin Johnston to make photographs of the building's condition. This is her record of the vestibule, its walls dark with grime, paint scaling, wine bottles littering the closet, a door installed in the stair hall opening.

*Johnston*

The vestibule as restored, with marble tiles relaid over a concrete floor, the arched doorway reopened.

*Chamowitz*

The entrance door and vestibule after basic cleaning but before restoration. The room was wood-floored at this time. For the left-side door opening, the big lock box was turned upside-down—a common practice in early America    *Johnston*

up in the term "style," which is not to be confused with cosmetic embellishment.

The style of the Octagon and some of its contemporaries expressed an American urge to stand clear of anything reminiscent of the England that had abused its colonies, and to develop towns that were American in appearance and spirit. The Octagon is one of the early statements of the first distinctly American architectural style, one that broke after the Revolution with the formality and the emphatic ornament of the Georgian manner in favor of a more open and approachable kind of building. It could be argued that it represented another departure, from the traditions embodied in the transplanted English manor houses of the colonial tobacco grandees, aloof in their domains, subject to hardly any law but their own, and viewed by other colonials as beings in little worlds apart from the exigencies of community life.

The usual American term for this style is "Federal." It is directly identified with Robert Adam, who practiced in England but was associated with a kind of Englishness with which Americans could negotiate. This is not a facade architecture, for it was designed from the inside out. It was basic Adam doctrine, which he had assimilated in turn from Neo-classic ideals, that there should be good reasons for putting rooms in certain arrangements, and that putting a room on

The kitchen's original herringbone brick floor was found under a concrete slab. Furniture and implements are of the 1800 period.  *Barrett*

one side just to balance a room on the other side was not a good enough reason. The test was that the arrangement serve useful and congenial purposes.

In its street demeanor, the Octagon displays a dignified reticence. The window sills are light accents in the clean expanses of red brick walls. Instead of stone lintels, prominent features of Georgian walls, the windows are topped with flat arches of rubbed face brick laid flush with the wall and making subdued contrasts of texture. The only wall enrichment is in the white stone panels inset between the second and third-story windows, the string course at the foot of curved iron balconies outside each second-story window, and a stone basement wall. The brick is laid in Flemish bond in the front walls, English bond in the rear.

Inside, the openness of plan encourages movement within well-connected spaces, the contrasting forms of Thornton's geometry. The decorative details of the plaster cornices and ceiling centerpieces, and of the window and door trims and chair rails, are scaled to enliven their surroundings like the stimulus of good conversation—they contribute but do not dominate. It takes close inspection to discover the abundant repertory of foliations, meanders, classical motifs and moldings in the plaster, and the virtuoso projections and undercutting in the woodwork, turned out by the craftsmen-carpenters with their molding planes.

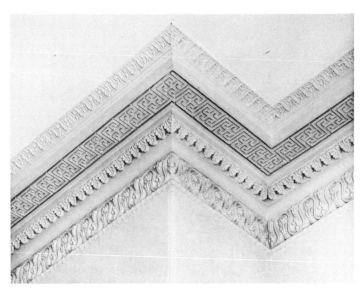

A section of drawing room cornice done by Gus Rubino in 1954 restoration. Original cornice was lost in all first-floor rooms when second-story floors were rebuilt.　*Chamowitz*

This style developed an American equilibrium and momentum that made it one of our most successful models of a design that could be clustered or joined in rows to make harmonious blocks in the fast-growing cities, or could stand alone with a sociable elegance.

It is remarkable that the Tayloe family encompassed the salient features of the Georgian esthetic in Mount Airy, and then followed this in the next generation with an outstanding Federal statement in the Octagon.

During AIA ownership, there has been hardly a year without a showing of repair and replacement of deteriorated parts. In the 43 years of the Octagon's minimal maintenance after the death of Mrs. Tayloe, and its tenancy finally with slum density, it suffered only superficial damage. There was not a chip missing from the Coade chimney pieces, and the other decoration was brought out from under its layers of grime and scaling paint in excellent condition. What had to be dealt with eventually were afflictions of age, but it was many years before this became urgent. There were two periods of major structural restoration, the first 1949–56, the second 1968–70.

In its first 10 years the AIA added two adjacent lots to the property, and carried out repairs necessary to protect the building and make it serve immediate headquarters office needs. These included new drains, roof work, relaying of the Eighteenth Street garden wall, and pointing of brick work in the cellar, window lightwells and the tunnel vault. The first interior structural rehabilitation was to remove the old joists under the entrance vestibule, pour an 8-inch concrete slab and relay the marble tiles. A few missing squares were replaced with similar tiles that had been removed from the old Treasury Building.

The Institute did not then need all the rooms, and for some years it had

Temporary stairway bracing, early in the AIA occupancy. Later a 2½-inch deflection was found at the second-floor landing, from where this photograph was taken.

*Johnston*

Main bedroom on the Eighteenth
Street side after the years of
tenement residency (*left*). The
same corner of this room (*Below*)
as it appears today, restored
and now used as an exhibition
gallery.     *Johnston / Barrett*

Tayloe family maple settee and matching arm chairs were brought back to the Octagon for grouping in the stair hall. The drawing room is to the left, dining room right, the entrance vestibule ahead.  *Barrett*

tenants. In 1915, the American Federation of Arts, the Archaeological Institute of America, the Washington Archaeological Society and the Washington Society of Fine Arts, among others, all were headquartered in the Octagon.

It became necessary that the AIA determine its long-range intentions as to the Octagon, and in 1914 it resolved that all work on the property, including the grounds, should be of the character of restoration to the condition of a town house of a gentleman of 1800. The members repeatedly emphasized in ensuing years a preference for keeping the house in service rather than to make it a house museum, although some museum activities have almost always been a part of its operation. For a time the Institute reserved a room or two as a members' club lounge and grill, but the tendency of rehabilitation was toward making the house serviceable again, with a faithful regard for its historic character.

As the basic reference for restoration then and in the future, Glenn Brown was assigned in 1914 to make measured drawings of the Octagon, and these were published in a large monograph of limited edition, which included ornament detail, molding profiles and other carefully drawn records of Thornton's design features.

By 1918 a hot-air furnace had been installed to serve part of the house, the doors and windows weather-stripped, the stable's front wall reinforced with tie rods, a sprinkler system installed throughout the house, the fireplaces and flues overhauled and some plastering and painting done.

At that time the AIA had been in possession long enough to begin repairing some of its own improvements on the heating plant and roof. The Treaty Room floor and the stairway hall floors were scraped and refinished. In 1924 the hot-air furnace was replaced with a steam system, the "radiators placed as inconspicuously as possible." The gas lighting system was disconnected and the building wired. Temporary girders and wood posts were placed in the kitchen to support the sagging dining room floor above.

The dining room floor was permanently reinforced with two steel beams in 1926, a job that required "changing many pipes and wires." The old brick floor in the kitchen was repaired, and the walls and ceiling were replastered.

By the 1930s the Institute's offices were beginning to be crowded in the Octagon, and construction of a new administration building was begun along the inner property lines, with a garden between this building and the Octagon. Its completion in 1940 coincided with a government need for emergency office space, and the new building was pre-empted for the Inter-American Defense Board, a function of the Department of State.

This left the AIA administrative staff in a state of increasing congestion, and the Octagon's venerable structure heavily loaded with the paraphernalia of a large headquarters operation. The administration department was in the drawing room, with the receptionist's desk and switchboard at the door. The dining room was used for mail and shipping, and as stock room for the contract documents that the organization sells to its members. The executive director's office was in the Treaty Room, and in other second-floor space were the membership files and the editor of the Journal of the American Institute of Architects with his secretary and backfiles. On the third floor were the accounting department and other office space. It was October 13, 1949, when the staff moved across the garden into its nine-year-old "new" headquarters. The Journal editor and the custodian were left in the Octagon as guardians.

Now restoration could proceed untrammeled by conflicts with office operations, except that during the World War II years and the remainder of the emergency period, work was limited to urgent repairs involving non-critical materials. Deteriorated Aquia Creek sandstone in the basement wall and in the second-floor string course was cut out to a depth of four inches and replaced with carefully matched stone from a Berea, Ohio, quarry. The brick foundation of the front steps was found to have crumbled into rubble—an unexpected repair expense of $1,053.

The restoration board reported to the 1950 convention that "After long effort and the expenditure of considerable funds the Octagon has finally been repaired and decorated to capture the dignity and charm which the building had when it was first built, 150 years ago." What the board thought was just about the final cost of restoration and repair was given in the report:

| | |
|---|---|
| Exterior walls | $29,018.54 |
| Interior repair & painting | 7,350.65 |
| Heating & electrical work | 12,882.94 |
| Furnishings | 12,049.12 |

The total came to $61,301.25.

There had been a false start in furnishing the house with reproductions, and in 1951 the restoration committee was directed to plan a more authentic treatment,

The dining room Coade chimney piece as the AIA found it (*right*), fitted with coal grate and decorated with wine bottles, and as it is now. The painting, by an unknown artist after Edward Savage, shows George and Martha Washington at Mount Vernon with the L'Enfant Plan; standing are Mrs. Washington's grandchildren, John Parke Custis and Nelly Custis, Mrs. Tayloe's friend. (Pennsylvania Academy of Fine Arts). *Johnston / Barrett*

Three stages of the chimney
piece in the master bedroom, now
usually called the Dolley Madison
Room: (*Left*) Just before AIA occupancy,
the fireplace crudely closed, and the
room heated by a coal stove, beside
which a barefoot boy sits on a
camp stool. (*Below*) In excellent condition after cleaning early in this century,
the coal grate about as it was in Mrs.
Tayloe's last years. (*Right*) Restored,
with full fireplace opening, a replacement hearth slab.

*Johnston / Chamowitz*

room by room in the display areas. James L. Cogar, an antiques specialist who had been active in the Colonial Williamsburg restorations, interviewed members of the Tayloe family at Mount Airy and other locations. With this and other research, he drew up floor plans with lists of appropriate furniture and its placement, and prepared cost estimates of American and English pieces of the 1800 period.

Because costs kept going up, the AIA continued for four years to rent tenant space for light use, limited to three persons in each large room, two in the smaller ones. The master bedroom on the New York Avenue side, usually called the Dolley Madison Room, was rented to the new National Council for Historic Sites and Buildings and the newly chartered National Trust for Historic Preservation. In 1952, the American Federation of Arts took over this room for a second stay in the Octagon, and was succeeded by the AIA group insurance staff. In other rooms were the staffs of the National Architectural Accrediting Board, a local Red Cross unit, and what later became the Modular Building Standards Association.

Late in 1953 the stable was converted to attractive reading rooms and stack space for the Institute's library, with a corridor connection to the administration building. This use was continued until both structures were removed for the present administration building.

In that year the Institute addressed itself to a problem that had been making it uneasy since 1949, when it was noticed that the main stairs were somewhat below alignment with the second floor. William Dewey Foster, consulting architect for the AIA in the renovation of the first two floors, conferred about the deflection with Milton L. Grigg, chairman of the Buildings and Grounds Committee, and Robert E. Lee, an engineer, who were restoring Thomas Jefferson's Monticello, and with James M. Gongwer, another engineer. The seriousness of the problem could be determined only by tests of the structure, so the Octagon was closed to the public and its floor and stairway supports examined.

Gongwer reported that the old floor timbers were showing as much stress under dead load alone as the values for good timbers under dead and live loads combined. (Dead load is the weight of the building components, live load the weight of occupants and furnishings.) Floor joists, which had lost muscle tone as a result of old age, had been further weakened by cutting for underfloor passage of plumbing pipes, electrical conduits and gas lines.

The stairway deflection at the second-floor level was 2½ inches. "Despite the legendary skill of our early builders," wrote Henry H. Saylor in a summation of repair work, "the header joist was a single one, 3" x 10". Moreover the curved casing covering the wall side needed a little more vertical space, so the side of the joist was chiseled off to a depth of a half inch or so after being set."

To re-establish the stairway, its weight was transferred to a cage of 8-by-8 upright timbers in a 1954 project. The plaster soffit and original wood lath were removed, and the wall stringers (framing members) disengaged. The stairway was inched up by jacks and wedges, then refastened to the walls. A 10-inch I-beam supported by upright 8-inch steel channels imbedded in the partition walls took the place of the weakened header. The stairway was replaced in proper relationship to the three floor levels without a crack in skirting, balusters or continuous handrail. It was found that iron balusters, placed at regular intervals and firmly joined to the rail, had contributed to its rigidity.

Floor joists and beams were found to be weak at the critical points where their ends rested in exterior brickwork or interior partition walls, and this raised the question of how important it was to conscientious restoration to conserve the wood substructure—considering the kind of bone-surgery reinforcement that would be necessary to do so. The determination was that the visible rooms had higher priority than the invisible structure. This cleared the way for steel and concrete, provided that the thickness of the floor, measured from ceiling plaster to the finished floor above, not vary a fraction of an inch from the old work.

Strengthening the first floor was fairly routine. The drawing room floor was adequately braced with a single lally column (a steel tube filled with cement) under the middle girder in the basement. The 1926 steel beams under the dining room floor were now augmented with diagonal members that spread the load through the old frame, which was left in place. The first floor was found to be a remarkable lattice of a transverse middle girder, 11 by 13 inches, in each room, crossed by four 5-by-7 beams running the length of the rooms. These were crossed by 4-by-4 joists parallel with the girder in two sets, running above and below an inner layer of planking on which was a deposit of material that seemed to be clay—for soundproofing.

The second-story floor was much more grave a problem, for there was no way to reinforce it. That meant that the floor structure had to be removed and rebuilt. On the under side of this floor structure was attached, of course, the first-story ceiling—and those beautifully wrought plaster cornices in the drawing room, the dining room and the stair hallway. The cornices in the vestibule were not involved because the Treaty Room above it was to be roped off as a museum space, and its floor not rebuilt. All the other cornices around the first-floor ceilings would be destroyed.

Those convinced that the old-time craftsmen have vanished are unaware of the role played by Gus Rubino in the 1954 restoration work. An Italian artist in fine plaster, Rubino selected a two-foot section of each cornice, cleaned it of accumulated paint and kept it as a model for casting new cornices. None of his younger helpers was even permitted to mount the scaffolding. Rubino did the cleaning, removing, duplicating and remounting. This was the last step of the new installation.

The floor had been rebuilt with a cellular structure of 16-gauge steel pans supported on heavy steel angles bolted to the walls. Tapered pine sleepers were bolted between the pans at 18-inch intervals; a lightweight concrete was poured flush with the tops of the sleepers, and the flooring nailed to them. The flooring in the Dolley Madison Room and in the stair hall is the original pine. Not enough of it could be salvaged for the room on the other side, and it was floored in new southern pine 1⅜ inches thick, in random widths, milled in Arkansas.

The removal of an old added partition just inside the dining room door to the stair hall revealed a small wall area and some woodwork that showed promise of having original paint. Some overlaying coats were painstakingly stripped down to a soft green of plaster and off-white woodwork. This combination was adopted for the dining room, with the stair hall in yellow and drawing room in off-white. The Treaty Room was given a white ceiling, and the walls papered and stippled in a dark green leathery texture.

It was at about this point that the bills began trickling up to the executive committee, and Saylor made a dry notation in his restoration report:

> *In view of the widespread experience of architects with costs that rise beyond preliminary estimates, it is rather surprising that the executive committee was annoyed by the executive director's report in June, 1955, that the original estimate of the Octagon reconstruction, $40,000, was now to be $47,500. Architect Foster was rebuked for not letting the Institute know the extent of the over-run at an earlier date.*

This was another of the moments when it seemed that reconstruction had been concluded, but one more stage of major reinforcement and restoration was yet to come. The program for use of the Octagon combined museum, exhibition, education, social and curatorial activities in its updated planning. The third floor was needed for staff work, meetings and exhibition preparations, but its use was severely limited by the still weak upper structure. Visitor restrooms were needed, serving pantries for staff and caterers, and year-around temperature and humidity control.

For years the AIA had hoped to establish an endowment for the Octagon's repairs and maintenance, and a number of committees had explored fund-raising possibilities. It finally became certain that this approach was unpromising, and in 1968 the Octagon was purchased for about $1,000,000 raised by subscriptions by the American Institute of Architects Foundation, a nonprofit corporation created by the Institute. It was the Foundation that directed the second major stage of restoration, begun in 1968 with J. Everette Fauber Jr. as the architect.

By this time preservation professionalism had come of age. Before any more work was undertaken, an architectural historian, Samuel Allen Chambers Jr., was assigned to search family records, public archives, municipal files, church records, newspaper files and libraries for background references to the Octagon, and to the Tayloe family during its period of construction and occupancy.

An archeological team was engaged to make digs around the outside walls in search of Tayloe artifacts (the area beyond having been disturbed by other construction, with loss of research value). Measured drawings and photographs recorded any evidence that came to light.

The original herringbone brick floor in the basement kitchen was repaired and, with removal of a concrete slab, sections of the same paving were uncovered in a closet off the kitchen, in a storeroom and in the wine vault, which is beneath the first-floor vestibule. The barrel-vaulted cells where wine kegs were stored on their sides were repaired, and several basement fireplaces reopened. The kitchen was equipped with utensils of John Tayloe's lifetime, including a spit-jack operated by weights. These were gifts as a memorial to Henry H. Saylor FAIA, whose devotion to the Octagon and its restoration had been a personal cause.

The service stairway was cleared of sprinkler piping, and reinforced. On the second floor, two fireplaces that had been removed from the large exhibition gallery room on the Eighteenth Street side (originally two bedrooms) were restored with their original mantelpieces. Two original arched recesses, flanking the fireplace in the end wall, had been removed in earlier work; they were put back.

Adjoining the Dolley Madison bedroom was originally a small room that presumably served the Tayloes as nursery and dressing room. It had been removed in converting the bedroom to a gallery, and now it was reinstated, along with the little hall leading to both these rooms. The bedchamber still serves as a gallery.

It was necessary to come to grips with the long avoided problem of the Treaty Room, which was showing a ceiling deflection. The commodious third-floor room above it, to which this ceiling was attached, was needed for meetings and work on exhibition materials. The other four large rooms on this floor, originally family bedrooms and quarters for chambermaids, were needed as headquarters for the AIA Foundation, and for curatorial offices, a library and storage. The entire third story had been condemned for occupancy some years before by the municipal Department of Licenses and Inspections, and the floor had to be replaced to meet building code standards. This was the most extensive structural change to be made within the building; it was accomplished with a combination of steel I-beams and heavy subflooring throughout this floor area.

Here the restorers achieved their finest hour: The Treaty Room ceiling plaster was skillfully cut away from the margins of the 1800 plaster cornice, which was left undisturbed while the rest of that room's ceiling, with the flooring structure of the room above it, was removed and replaced. Then the ceiling was replastered and rejoined to the cornice.

A hard decision was whether to restore Thornton's flat roof. There were three influential points: The change to a pitched roof had been made in Tayloe's lifetime; there was the hazard that the flat roof would be as impractical again as it had been in the first place, and the attic space was needed for climate control equipment.

The pitched roof was covered with fire-rated cypress shingles to match as nearly as possible the first shingles found under the terne roof, and in the attic were installed two large fan coil units, with the controls and duct work of electric heating and cooling equipment for the second and third floors. Two other fan coil units were put in the basement servants' rooms and in the "tunnel," to serve the basement and first floor. All are on isolator mountings that prevent the transmission of any noise or vibration to the building structure. Ducts were unobtrusively threaded through closet spaces, fireplace flues and walls, with discreetly placed outlets. The restoration of plaster and woodwork was done with care to match adjacent patinas.

The Octagon was designated a National Historic Landmark in 1961, and at last, in January, 1970, it was in condition to be fully occupied, with its principal

American Institute of Architects headquarters ensemble—the Octagon and the Administration Building. A pen and ink drawing by John Desmond, FAIA.

The Octagon, with recently constructed brick curbing and oak trees. The new AIA
Administration Building is beyond. It extends from New York Avenue (*right*) to Eighteenth
Street in a long curve that encloses a paved terrace and a garden, between the two buildings.

*Barrett*

rooms opened to public view as historic interiors of the Federal period, and its two second-floor galleries commited to an exhibition program of historic and contemporary architectural material. In 1972 the Octagon was accredited by the American Association of Museums.

The collection of furnishings has grown in quality and authenticity, and the Foundation continues to seek furnishings, memorial objects and contributions. Some Tayloe Octagon pieces have come home again, by gift or purchase. On the first floor these include a maple settee and matching chairs in the stair hall, a three-part Sheffield plateau that is displayed on the dining table on special occasions, and family porcelains.

As a memorial gift from the family of John W. Cross FAIA, of New York, the dining room received its Hepplewhite table and chairs, an inlaid mahogany sideboard for the shallow wall recess and a Scottish breakfront.

In the Treaty Room, the leather-bound casket in which the Treaty of Ghent was delivered to President Madison rests on Colonel Tayloe's pivoted circular English rent table, made of mahogany with wedge-shaped drawers marked from A to Z in ivory inlay. This table, one of several Tayloe pieces in the room, has had an adventurous existence. Following its presumed role in the treaty-signing episode and further use by the Octagon family, it eventually was inherited by John Ogle Tayloe, of King George County, Virginia, who sold it in 1897 to Mrs. A. H. Voorhies of San Franciso. When the 1906 earthquake and fire threatened her home on California Street, Mrs. Voorhies wrapped the table in bedsheets and rolled it like a wheel out of danger. Later she loaned the table for exhibition at an AIA convention in San Francisco, and then sold it for $1,000 to that city's AIA chapter, which returned it to the Octagon in 1911. Now it stands in the center of the room on a circular Axminster rug of Adam design, a 1952 gift.

The 1940 administration building was demolished in 1971 for construction of the seven-story, $7,000,000 headquarters of concrete aggregate and glass that now extends in a long curve between the two streets. It is the design of The Architects Collaborative, and it succeeded a competition-winning design by Mitchell/ Giurgola Associates that was rejected by the Commission of Fine Arts as "being out of keeping with the Octagon House," among other objections that stirred spirited controversy.

There was an old custom of putting a little ivory "amity button" in a cusp at the tip of the newel post when a house had been satisfactorily completed and paid for. One had been placed in the center of each spiral of the Octagon stairway railings on the first floor, but they were lost in the time of trouble. The replacement buttons signify the beginning of new life. They betoken the completion of a restoration that was vastly more complicated and costly than the American Institute of Architects had imagined when it rented the Octagon for $30 a month, but which set exemplary standards for zeal, perseverance, conviction and quality.

Elevations of parlor walls, and details of its ceiling centerpiece, cornice, window and door trim, window and door panels, and chair rail. *Brown.*

 THE OCTAGON

# SELECTED
# BIBLIOGRAPHY

Brown, Glenn. *The Octagon: Dr. William Thornton, Architect.* Washington: The American Institute of Architects, 1914.

————. *History of the United States Capitol.* Washington: U.S. Government Printing Office, 1900 (2 vol.)

Bruce, Philip Alexander. *Institutional History of Virginia in the Seventeenth Century.* New York and London: G. P. Putnam's Sons, The Knickerbocker Press, 1910. (2 vol.)

Butler, Jeanne F. *Competition 1792: Designing a Nation's Capitol.* Foreword by George M. White. Special issue of "Capitol Studies," U.S. Capitol Historical Society, Vol. 4, No. 1. (Catalogue of design exhibition at the Octagon.)

Cable, Mary. *The Avenue of the Presidents.* Boston: Houghton Mifflin Co., 1969.

Caemmerer, Hans Paul. *Washington, the National Capital.* Washington: U.S. Government Printing Office, 1932.

Cox, Warren J.; Jacobsen, Hugh Newell; Lethbridge, Francis D.; and Rosenthal, David R., for the Washington Metropolitan Chapter of the American Institute of Architects. *A Guide to the Architecture of Washington, D.C.* 2nd ed. New York: McGraw-Hill Book Co., 1974.

Craven, Wesley Frank. *Dissolution of the Virginia Company; the Failure of a Colonial Experiment.* Gloucester, Mass.: P. Smith, 1964.

"Decatur House." Historic Preservation, Vol. 19, 3–4. (July–December), 1967. Washington: National Trust for Historic Preservation.

Dickens, Charles, *American Notes.* Introduction by Christopher Lasch. Gloucester, Mass.: P. Smith, 1968.

Eskew, Garnett Laidlaw. *Willard's of Washington: The Epic of a Capital Caravansary.* Assisted by B. P. Adams. New York: Coward-McCann, 1954.

Fauber, J. Everette Jr. "A Comprehensive Report Leading to the Restoration of the Octagon in Washington, D.C." Unpublished report to the Octagon Committee and the Executive Board of the American Institute of Architects. (Includes comprehensive bibliography of Octagon and Tayloe family materials.) Washington: The American Institute of Architects Library, 1968.

Federal Writers' Program, American Guide Series. *Virginia, a Guide to the Old Dominion.* 5th ed. New York: Oxford University Press, 1952.

Fithian, Philip Vickers. *The Journal and Letters of Philip Vickers Fithian, 1773–1774: A Plantation Tutor of the Old Dominion.* Williamsburg, Va.: Colonial Williamsburg, Inc., 1965; distributed by the University Press of Virginia.

Foster, Sir Augustus John. *Jeffersonian America.* Edited by Richard Beale Davis. San Marino, Calif.: Huntington Library, 1954.

Halbig, Harriet Portner; Pettengill, George E.; and Fauber, J. Everette Jr. *The Octagon: Restoring a Landmark.* Washington: The American Institute of Architects Foundation, 1974. (Catalogue of an exhibition at the Octagon.)

Howells, John Mead. *Lost Examples of Colonial Architecture.* 2nd ed. New York: Dover Publications, 1963.

Kimball, Fiske. *Domestic Architecture of the American Colonies and of the Early Republic.* 2nd ed. New York: Dover Publications, 1966.

King, George Harrison Sanford. *Marriages of Richmond County, Virginia, 1668–1853.* (Mimeographed.) Fredericksburg, Va., 1964.

Lord, Walter. *The Dawn's Early Light.* New York: W. W. Norton, 1972.

Myer, Donald Beekman. *Bridges and the City of Washington.* Washington: U.S. Commission of Fine Arts, 1974. (Catalogue of an exhibition at the Octagon.)

Pearce, Mrs. John N. (Revised by William V. Elder III.) *The White House: An Historic Guide.* Washington: White House Historical Association, 1963.

Pierson, William H. Jr. *American Buildings and Their Architects: The Colonial and Neo-classical Styles.* Garden City, N.Y.: Doubleday & Co., 1970.

*Records of the Virginia Company of London.* The Court Book, from the manuscript in the Library of Congress. Washington: U.S. Government Printing Office, 1906. (4 vol.)

Reiff, Daniel D. *Washington Architecture, 1791–1861.* Washington: U.S. Commission of Fine Arts, 1971.

Reps, John W. *Monumental Washington: The Planning and Development of the Capital Center.* Princeton, N.J.: Princeton University Press, 1967.

Saylor, Henry H. "The Octagon: Restoration of 1947–1956." Unpublished summary of the official discussions, sketches, working drawings, correspondence and other material relating to the restoration. Washington: American Institute of Architects Library, 1963.

Talpalar, Morris. *The Sociology of Colonial Virginia.* New York: Philosophical Library, 1960.

Tayloe Family Papers, University of Virginia Library, Charlottesville, on loan from Edward Thornton Tayloe, Charlottesville.

Tayloe Family Papers, Virginia Historical Society, Richmond, the gift of Colonel Henry Gwynne Tayloe Jr., Mount Airy.

Tayloe, W. Randolph. *The Tayloes of Virginia and Allied Families.* (Mimeographed.) Berryville, Va., 1963.

Whiffen, Marcus. *American Architecture Since 1780: A Guide to the Styles.* Cambridge, Mass.: MIT Press, 1969.

———. *The Eighteenth-Century Houses of Williamsburg.* Williamsburg: Colonial Williamsburg, Inc., distributed by Holt, Rinehart and Winston, New York, 1960.

Yerkes, David N. FAIA. *William Thornton: A Renaissance Man in the Federal City,* American Institute of Architects Foundation, 1976.

# THE SONS AND DAUGHTERS OF
# JOHN TAYLOE III (1771–1828) AND
# ANNE OGLE TAYLOE (1772–1855)

1. JOHN TAYLOE IV, born August 2, 1793, at the home of his maternal grandparents, Annapolis; married to Maria Forrest, daughter of Colonel Uriah Forrest of General Washington's staff; promoted to lieutenant in the United States Navy for heroism in the War of 1812; died at Mount Airy May 15, 1824. Burial on the plantation.

2. HENRIETTA HILL TAYLOE, born December 4, 1794, at Annapolis; married June 20, 1815, to H.G.S. Key of Maryland; died June 11, 1832, at Tudor Hall, Maryland. (Key was brother to Francis Scott Key, who in 1814 wrote "The Star-Spangled Banner"; Francis Scott Key married Henrietta's cousin, Mary Tayloe Lloyd, whose mother, Elizabeth Tayloe, was the first child of John Tayloe II.)

3. BENJAMIN OGLE TAYLOE, born May 21, 1796, at Annapolis; married November 8, 1824, to Julia Maria Dickinson of Troy, New York, who died July 4, 1846; second marriage to Phoebe Warren of Troy; Benjamin Ogle Tayloe died February 25, 1868, at Rome, Italy. Burial at Troy.

4. REBECCA PLATER TAYLOE, born September 7, 1797, at Annapolis; unmarried; died March 24, 1815, at Mount Airy. Burial at Mount Airy.

5. WILLIAM HENRY TAYLOE, born January 27, 1799, at Mount Airy; married May 4, 1824, to Henrietta Ogle, daughter of his maternal uncle, Benjamin Ogle II of Bel Air, Maryland; died April 10, 1871, at Georgetown. Inherited Mount Airy.

6. ANNE TAYLOE, born March 23, 1800, at Annapolis; died April 23, 1800.

7. CATHERINE CARTER TAYLOE II, born April 1, 1801, at Mount Airy; married May 18, 1824, to James Baker of London, then British assistant consul general in Washington; died at Barcelona, Spain.

8. EDWARD THORNTON TAYLOE, born January 31, 1803, at the Octagon; married December 16, 1830, to his cousin Mary Ogle (sister of Mrs. William Henry Tayloe); died in December, 1876, at Powhatan, the house he completed in 1832 in King George County.

9. GEORGE PLATER TAYLOE, born October 15, 1804, at Mount Airy; married October 14, 1830, to Mary Elizabeth Langhorne, daughter of William Langhorne of Botetourt County; built the mansion Buena Vista at Roanoke, now owned and preserved by that city; died 1897.

10. ELIZABETH MERRY TAYLOE, born March 21, 1806, at the Octagon; married May 11, 1829, to her first cousin, Robert Wormeley Carter II of Sabine Hall, a mansion of about 1735 near Mount Airy; died in Washington March 21, 1832. Carter's mother was Catherine Tayloe, daughter of John Tayloe II, and his father was Landon Carter II.

11. HENRY AUGUSTINE TAYLOE, born in 1808 at the Octagon; married April 19, 1838, to Narcissa Jamieson, daughter of John and Virginia (Adair) Jamieson of Alabama; they resided at Gallion, Hale County, Alabama; died 1903 in Washington.

12. CHARLES TAYLOE, born Feb. 15, 1810, at the Octagon; married August 3, 1831, to Virginia Anne Turner of King George County, daughter of Richard Turner.

13. VIRGINIA TAYLOE, born July 23, 1813, at the Octagon; unmarried; died April 5, 1883, at Baltimore, where she had resided.

14. ANNE OGLE TAYLOE, born August 11, 1814, at the Octagon; married at the Octagon November 30, 1841, to Henry Howell Lewis, who became a captain in the Confederate States Navy, and was a great great nephew of George Washington; she died July 25, 1876, at Baltimore, where she had resided.

15. LLOYD TAYLOE, born November 8, 1815, at the Octagon; died August 8, 1816.

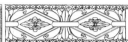  

# INDEX

**Denotes illustration**

Composed in Linotype Palatino by Monotype Composition Company, Inc., Baltimore
Printed on Mohawk Navajo by The John D. Lucas Co., Baltimore
Designed by Gerard Valerio